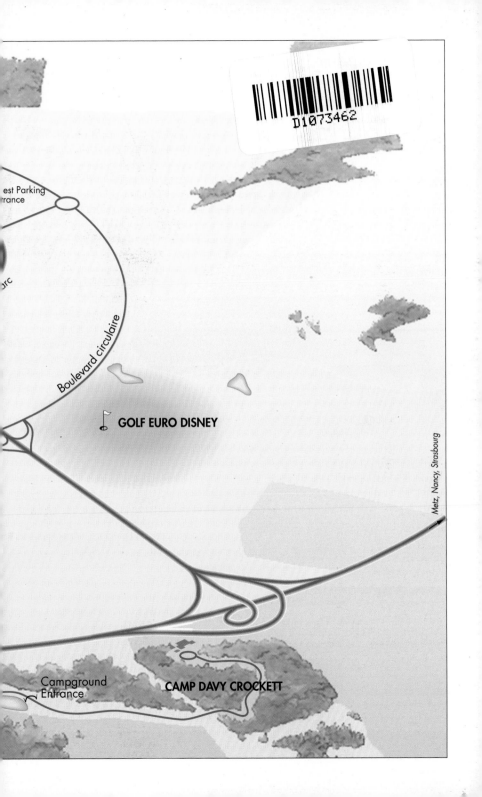

THE GUIDE

This book was conceived and produced collectively,
under the initiative and direction of the European Creative Center, by

BOOKMAKER

with

MARIE-ALICE CHICOU, RÉGINE FERRANDIS
(editorial coordination)
VÉRONIQUE CELTON
(production)
MAGGIE DOYLE, KHIA MASON, CLIO MITCHELL, WILLIAM SNOW
(writers)

and

D.A. GRAPHISME - DANIEL ARNAULT (graphic layout) with MONIQUE ARMANT
FRANÇOIS HUERTAS
(cover)
GILLES ALKAN with PHILIPPE BOUTET and PHILIPPE MALAUSSÉNA
(maps)
ATELIER PHILIPPE HARCHY
(illustration)
HERVÉ BOUTET, FRED CAROL, JEAN-CLAUDE FIGENWALD,
VINCENT GODEAU, GARY KRUEGER, VINCENT LELOUP,
CHRISTIAN MALETTE, JEAN-CHRISTOPHE MOREAU,
ÉRIC MORENCY, PHILIPPE ROLLE
(photography)
and the WALT DISNEY WORLD RESORT and DISNEYLAND PARK photographers.

BOOKMAKER and WALT DISNEY CONSUMERS PRODUCTS wish to extend
special thanks to ANNE WEINER, WENDY WOLFE et CRAIG FLEMING.

THE GUIDE

TABLE OF CONTENTS

*Creating a new Disney Resort in Europe has been
The Walt Disney Company's most important project in this decade.
From the very beginning we've been lucky to have many
great people involved in the project, in particular the Imagineers,
those engineers of the imagination who have once
again transformed our dreams into reality.
We're happy to be part of a new Europe and to offer our European
guests the chance to discover a thrilling family
vacation resort and the best of all Disney theme parks.
This guidebook will give you the keys
to enter the new magical kingdom of Disney.*

MICHAEL EISNER

*When I look at the Euro Disneyland Park, and in particular
at the château, I'm reminded of the marvelous images
created for the animated film, Sleeping Beauty, and I'm proud to say that
the Château de la Belle au Bois Dormant is the most spectacular
fantasy castle ever built for a Disney Park... and what
better place for it than in the country of Charles Perrault?
For my family and me, it is exciting that our classic
characters, some created by Walt, some taken from the pages
of European fairy tales, now have such a wonderful home.
In conclusion, I would like to wish you all an
exciting and unforgettable stay at the Euro Disney Resort
and thank you for sharing in our dream!*

ROY DISNEY

*Here at Disney, we believe in miracles,
and when you believe in miracles – they happen!
Four years ago, Euro Disneyland was nothing
more than a mass of architect's drawings and blueprints.
Now, it's a full-fledged resort with
its own theme park, hotels, entertainment center,
campground, and golf course.
How did this miracle happen? Through the hard work
of thousands of people, from Cast Members and construction
workers to Imagineers, all of whom have infused the
Euro Disney Resort with their talent, energy, and passion.
Thanks to them, you'll have the privilege
of participating in the best show ever put on by Disney.
For a sneak preview, delve into this guidebook.*

ROBERT FITZPATRICK

ONCE UPON A TIME...

This particular story begins like a fairy-tale... Once upon a time, a proud father was sitting on a park bench munching on peanuts, as he watched a merry-go-round spinning round and round. He often took his two young daughters to the park, where they had lots of fun on those sunny Sunday afternoons. He, on the other hand, like the other parents sitting around him on benches, was bored to tears. "Why should parents be bored he mused, while their children are enjoying themselves?" He thought there ought to be a place where parents and their children could have fun together and he vowed to make his dream come true. The proud father was Walt Disney.

It all began with a Mouse. Walter Elias Disney was born on December 5, 1901 in Chicago, Illinois. His talent for drawing was discovered and developed at an early age. At the age of twenty-one, with only a few dollars in his pocket, he left his home and family in Kansas City, Missouri, and headed for Hollywood, California.

There, Walt began producing short animated films and on October 16, 1923, established the Disney Brothers Studios with his brother Roy. The prospects for the fledgling studio were marginal until the creation of Mickey Mouse in 1928. Mickey made his screen debut in *Steamboat Willie*, the first animated film with synchronized sound. The film established Mickey Mouse as an international star and put the Disney Brothers Studios on the

◄ *"What I want more than anything else is for Disneyland to be a place where people are happy, where children and grown-ups can have exhilarating experiences and fabulous times together and come out feeling the better for it."*

Walt and Roy Disney with young film buff.

13

Hollywood map. In 1929 Walt introduced the *Silly Symphonies*, a series of musical animated shorts, including the most popular film of the series, *The Three Little Pigs*. The series was widely acclaimed by the

Mickey Mouse... over 60 years of international success.

public and critics, and in 1932 Walt Disney won the first Academy Award ever awarded to an animated short film *(Flowers and Trees)*. In 1937 Walt Disney produced, at great financial and critical risk, the first feature-length animated film, *Snow White and the Seven Dwarfs*. The film became an international hit and began the legacy of the feature-length animated Disney classics.

But the Walt Disney Studios produced more than just animated features. Walt Disney had other interests, and he proceeded to produce his celebrated "True-Life Adventure" nature films including: *Seal Island* (1948), *The Living Desert* (1953), and *The Alaskan Eskimo* (1953). The Disney Studios also began producing live-action adventure films including *Treasure Island* (1950), *20,000*

The Disney Animated Classics

Snow White and the Seven Dwarfs was the precedent-setting film responsible for the 29 Disney feature-length animated films that have followed since 1937, and that have entertained millions of audiences world-wide:
Pinocchio and *Fantasia* (1940); *Dumbo* (1941); *Bambi* (1942); *Saludos Amigos* (1943); *The Three Caballeros* (1945); *Make Mine Music* (1946); *Fun and Fancy Free* (1947); *Melody Time* (1948); *The Adventures of Ichabod and Mr. Toad* (1949); *Cinderella* (1950); *Alice in Wonderland* (1951); *Peter Pan* (1953); *Lady and the Tramp* (1955); *Sleeping Beauty* (1959); *101 Dalmatians* (1961); *The Sword in the Stone* (1963); *The Jungle Book* (1967); *The Aristocats* (1970); *Robin Hood* (1973); *The Many Adventures of Winnie the Pooh* (1977); *The Rescuers* (1977); *The Fox and the Hound* (1981); *The Black Cauldron* (1985); *The Great Mouse Detective* (1986); *Oliver & Company* (1988); *The Little Mermaid* (1989); *The Rescuers Down Under* (1990); *Beauty and the Beast* (1991).

Leagues Under the Sea (1953), and *Davy Crockett, King of the Wild Frontier* (1955). Walt Disney was one of the early television pioneers with such award-winning programmes as the *Mickey Mouse Club* and *The Wonderful World of Disney*, much to the delight of television audiences.

A magical place. Walt Disney's creations have enchanted millions of people, both young and old, the world over. His philosophy consisted of a few very simple ideas. He believed in a better world where harmony, brotherhood and peace would reign.

His humanistic viewpoint with a utopian slant was founded on traditional values such as the family, which was sacrosanct for him; science, whose discoveries fascinated him; education; and respect for nature. In the early 1950s, a grand plan set his imagination and know-how in motion: he dreamed of creating a place where children and adults could share the same dream. In California in 1955, he opened the doors of his first theme park — the fabulous new realm of Disneyland Park. The overwhelming success of Disneyland Park inspired him to start developing an even more

Dream Makers

"You can dream up, design and build the most magical place in the world, but the magic won't work unless there are people to make the dream come true." Those people are the Imagineers and Cast Members, and as their unusual names indicate, they are the creators of an amazing imaginary world.

Established by Walt Disney in 1952 to create Disneyland Park in California, Walt Disney Imagineering is the master planning, creative development, design, engineering, production and project management subsidiary of The Walt Disney Company, responsible for the creation of the Disney Theme Parks and their expansion. The Imagineering team consists of a wide range of artists, designers, writers, technicians and administrators who create and build the most recognized theme park attractions in the world. Together, they are responsible for all phases of project development — from concept initiation to field art direction to attraction installation. At Euro Disneyland Park, Walt Disney Imagineering is responsible for the design and realization of the Theme Park and the concept and theming of the Disneyland Hotel marking its entrance.

As for the Cast Members, they are the actors in a show unlike any other you've seen. They make Walt Disney's dream of "making Disneyland the happiest land in the world" come true, welcoming and entertaining each and every guest as soon as a step is taken into the magical realm.

ambitious project, the creation of a complete holiday world. Walt Disney died on December 15, 1966, and thus never saw his dream come true. But his brother Roy and his other colleagues kept up the good work. In 1971 a new concept was born with the inauguration of the Walt Disney World Resort in Florida. The concept has now travelled to Europe with the creation of the Euro Disney Resort in 1992.

"Resort". The Euro Disney Resort is the epitome of a new concept. A resort is a place to spend a holiday, and the Euro Disney Resort brings a totally new dimension to the world of leisure and holidays, widening the scope to include a multitude of different kinds of accommodation and dining possibilities, as well as a variety of attractions designed for people of all ages and tastes.

The Euro Disney Resort is indeed an enormous holiday destination, consisting of six hotels, a camp-ground, a convention centre, an entertainment centre and a wide range of sports and leisure activities (featuring tennis courts, swimming pools, health clubs and a golf course). The Euro Disney Resort also contains a fabulous theme park built around five "lands": Main Street, U.S.A., the main street of an American town from the turn of the century; Frontierland, re-creating the Wild West; Adventure-land, with tropical islands, pirates and shipwrecks; Fantasyland, whose castle, Le Château de la Belle au Bois Dormant, is the symbol of Euro Disneyland Park, bringing to life childhood tales and legends; and Discoveryland, the land of the future as imagined by Leonardo da Vinci, Jules Verne and H.G. Wells.

France welcomes Mickey Mouse. France and Marne-la-Vallée were chosen for good reasons. The Paris region is situated in the heart of Europe, a crossroads for millions of tourists, making it a particularly attractive place to visit.

The transportation network is extremely well-developed, varied and modern. The two international airports, Orly and Roissy-Charles de Gaulle, both with multiple terminals, attract travellers from all over the world to Ile-de-France. The Euro Disney Resort is also situated next to the A4 motorway; and the Park is connected with Paris and its environs by a direct rail line through the RER (Regional Express Network). As of 1994 the TGV (High-Speed Train) will connect the Euro Disney Resort directly with Europe's railways. Ile-de-France's temperate climate was yet another reason for choosing Marne-la-Vallée.

And, as if all that weren't enough to justify choosing France as the site for the Euro Disney Resort, the name Disney happens to come from "d'Isigny", from the charming little village of Isigny-sur-Mer on the Normandy coast where the Disney family originally came from. So it's just like getting back to one's roots...

The European Disneyland Park. Fairy-tale characters such as Sleeping Beauty, Snow White and the Seven Dwarfs, Cinderella and Pinocchio, who have enchanted children all over the world via Walt Disney's classic motion picture adaptations, were originally created by European writers. Now they have come back to their homeland, gathering within the magical borders of Le Château de la Belle au Bois Dormant, whose design was partly influenced by illustrations from *Les Très Riches Heures du duc de Berry*. The medieval illuminated manuscripts of this book also influenced Disney artist Eyvind Earle's designs for the Walt Disney animated film classic, *Sleeping Beauty*, released in 1959, which also influenced the design of the castle. The heavenward-spiralling architecture of Mont St. Michel, a well-known French landmark, was also a major influence.

The fact that the Euro Disney Resort is being built in Europe has also given rise to several other specific creations. Alice's Curious Labyrinth, for instance, is in the tradition of maze gardens, and many of the themes developed in Discoveryland were inspired by the works of European visionaries such as Jules Verne and Leonardo da Vinci. Moreover, visual elements have been even more strongly stressed here because of the wide variety of languages spoken in Europe.

As with the other Parks, Euro Disneyland Park was conceived with Disney know-how; but groups from a variety of countries have come together to undertake the actual construction. For instance, the steamboats were built in France, many of the special effects were created in Germany and vehicles for some attractions were assembled in Italy.

A number of companies in Europe have sponsored attractions or shows, whereas others host restaurants or shops (see above box).

Towards the year 2017...

"I've always enjoyed working on projects that are full of life, and that continue to evolve and develop over time. Disneyland will never be finished, as long as there are people with imagination, with new dreams and new projects somewhere in the world." Walt Disney's words were prophetic.

> The following companies sponsor facilities within the Euro Disney Resort: American Express, BNP, Coca-Cola, Esso, Europcar, France Telecom, IBM, Kodak, Mattel, Nestlé, Philips and Renault.

The Euro Disney Resort certainly isn't lacking in new projects; its growth has been mapped out all the way until the year 2017. In the mid 1990s a new theme park will open, the Disney-MGM Studios - Europe, built around one of the great Hollywood studios. In the meantime, the Euro Disney Resort will have an additional 13,000 hotel rooms, a water-sports facility, a new convention centre, an expanded golf course and a larger campground.

Walt's projects just keep on growing. Thanks to his successors, who have remained faithful to his vision, the dream has become a reality.

PRACTICAL INFORMATION

How to use this guidebook

When to go

How to get there

- By car
- By RER
- By train
- By airplane
- By taxi

Arriving at the Euro Disney Resort

- By car
- By taxi
- By RER

Getting into the Park

Your Euro Disney Resort holiday

- A multifaceted resort
- Planning your holiday
- Accommodation
- Sports and leisure activities

Life at the Euro Disney Resort

- The locals
- Guests
- Languages
- Money
- Communications
- Some tips
- First aid
- Transportation
- Shopping
- Restaurants
- Shows
- Nightlife

How to use this guidebook

This guidebook gives you a thorough description of the Euro Disney Resort in great detail so that you can get the most out of the many kinds of accommodations, entertainment and leisure activities at your disposal.

• First of all you have the **practical information**. The Euro Disney Resort is a world unto itself, with its customs, means of communication, traditions and lifestyle... The table of contents for this section is found on p. 19.

• **Euro Disneyland Park** is presented from pps. 52 to 109 on easy-to-find pages with coloured edges.
A general map of the Euro Disneyland Park showing the five lands is followed by detailed information on each land, including:
– A map with a list of attractions, restaurants and shops marked by numbers.
– A precise description of each land in which attractions, restaurants and shops are introduced on a typical route that you might take. Symbols at the beginning of the text:

 for light refreshments

 for restaurants
with counter service

 for restaurants
with table service

 for attractions

 for shops

allow you to find what you're looking for at a glance, and the numbers inside the circles make it possible to locate them on the map of that land.

– Operating hours can be found in a box on p. 24.

– Descriptions of the various forms of entertainment you can see. When they take place at a specific restaurant or attraction, shows are described in the paragraph devoted to that locale. When they are itinerant, shows are listed in separate boxes at the end of the chapter devoted to each land.

• **The entertainment centre**, Festival Disney, has a whole chapter devoted to it, from pps. 110 to 117.

• **The hotels and campground** are presented on pps. 118 to 147.
– Prices and reservation information are presented in the practical information section on pps. 39 to 42.

• If you're interested in **Golf Euro Disney**, see pps. 148 to 149.

• There is also a **restaurant index**, classified according to the kind of meal served, see p. 151.

• Finally, the **general index**, arranged in alphabetical order, allows you to find attractions, restaurants, shops and any other information you may require, see pps. 152 to 157.

• There are 12 **maps** in this guidebook, presented in the following order:

General map of the Resort	at the front of the guidebook
Map of Euro Disneyland Park	pps. 52-53
Map of Main Street, U.S.A.	p. 56
Map of Frontierland	p. 70
Map of Adventureland	p. 80
Map of Fantasyland	p. 88
Map of Discoveryland	p. 102
Map of Festival Disney	pps. 110-111
Map of the hotel area	p. 119
Map of the campground	p. 144
Map of Euro Disneyland Park	at the end of the guidebook
Location map	on the back cover

Symbols on the maps indicate the various services available :

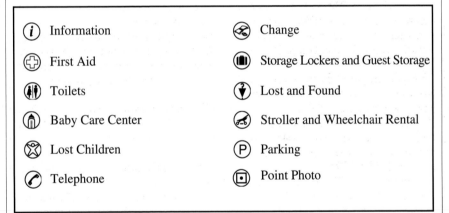

(i)	Information	(⊗)	Change
(✚)	First Aid	(▥)	Storage Lockers and Guest Storage
(⋔)	Toilets	(↓)	Lost and Found
(⌂)	Baby Care Center	(⇄)	Stroller and Wheelchair Rental
(⊗)	Lost Children	(P)	Parking
(✆)	Telephone	(▣)	Point Photo

The prices and operating hours listed in this guidebook are subject to change. Don't hesitate to ask for further information upon arrival or while making reservations. You may also call Guest Relations at (33-1) 64 74 30 00.

Despite the care taken in putting together this guidebook, it's possible that a piece of information has been omitted or has changed. We apologize for any inconvenience this may have caused you and welcome any comments you may have.

When to go

"What's the weather going to be like tomorrow?" Visitors at the Euro Disney Resort won't have to ask themselves that question, because everything has been planned for them to have a pleasant vacation at all times of year. The Euro Disneyland Park, Festival Disney and other attractions are perfectly adapted to Ile-de-France weather conditions.

Ile-de-France has a temperate climate, which is one of the main reasons it was chosen as the site for the Euro Disney Resort. Situated in the heart of Europe, Ile-de-France is not subject to the extreme temperatures that affect both Northern and Southern Europe. Winters are mild, with average temperatures above 0 °C (32 °F) even in January and February, when the weather is coldest. It is moderately warm in the summer but never stifling, with average temperatures around 25 °C (77 °F) in July and August. Changes of season are generally gradual, with mild and clear weather for three months in the spring and pleasant autumn weather that often lasts until the end of November. Moreover, Ile-de-France is subject neither to the droughts prevalent in certain areas of the continent in the summer nor to the constant dampness of coastal areas. In fact, annual rainfall is quite average, with regular periods of sunshine throughout the year. The mild climate is therefore ideally suited to the various outdoor activities offered at the Euro Disney Resort.

The Euro Disney Resort is open 365 days a year and everything has been designed so that visitors get the most out of their stay no matter what the weather. If need be, you can always buy one of the Mickey Mouse raincoats on sale at Plaza East and Plaza West Boutiques to the right and left of the Main Entrance and in many other shops of the Park.

Main Street, U.S.A., the land closest to the entrance to the Euro Disneyland Park, represents the main street of an American town at the turn of the century. Buildings with covered walkways in the style of the period line the street, and two arcades behind these buildings give on to the various shops and attractions. In Liberty Arcade, situated to the west of Main Street, there's an exhibition on the Statue of Liberty. In Discovery Arcade, located to the east of Main Street, famous inventions, drawings and plans for flying machines, cars and trains are on display. What better way to pass the time while sheltering from a shower?

The five lands of Euro Disneyland Park also include many attractions that are either indoors or sheltered from the rain. Likewise walkways, waiting areas, shops and shows in the Park are also "rainproof". Most restaurants have verandas, in addition to outdoor terraces, affording a pleasant view of the surroundings in a comfortable indoor setting.

Moreover, hotels, restaurants, shops, game rooms, cinemas, and indoor attractions are air-conditioned, considerably reducing the effects of changing weather. Swimming is possible all year round due to the indoor and outdoor pools in the hotels and campground. Winter sports are also available at the Euro Disney Resort. To the delight of skating enthusiasts, Rockefeller Plaza skating rink, located at Hotel New York, is open all winter long.

In summertime, the rink is converted into an ornamental pool with a fountain.

When to go to the Euro Disney Resort

School holidays (Christmas, Easter, July and August in the summer, and the week of Halloween, for France), national holidays, and long weekends are when you're likely to find the largest crowds at the Euro Disney Resort. We suggest that you visit the Euro Disney Resort during the autumn, winter and spring. In general, weekdays will be less crowded than weekends. To help you pick the best time of year for your visit, we've drawn up the following chart with information about attendance levels.

	LOWER ATTENDANCE	MODERATE ATTENDANCE	HEAVIER ATTENDANCE		LOWER ATTENDANCE	MODERATE ATTENDANCE	HEAVIER ATTENDANCE
JANUARY	After New Year's day		New Year's day and/or New Year's day weekend	JULY		1st and 2nd week	Weekdays and weekends of the last two weeks
FEBRUARY	Weekends and weekdays			AUGUST			Weekdays and weekends all month
MARCH	Weekends and weekdays			SEPTEMBER	Weekdays as of 2nd week	Weekends as of 2nd week	
APRIL		Weekdays	Weekends	OCTOBER	Weekdays up to last week	Weekends up to last week	Last week (Halloween)
MAY		Weekdays in mid-May	Beginning and end of May and weekends	NOVEMBER	As of 2nd November		
JUNE		Weekdays	Weekends	DECEMBER	Until week before Christmas	Week before Christmas	From Christmas to end of month

Planning how to spend your time is important in order to make the most of the many attractions offered at the Euro Disney Resort. It's true that crowds are at their peak during school and national holidays (see box p. 23). If you prefer to avoid large crowds, we recommend planning your visit during the autumn, winter or early spring. Don't forget that the Park is open every day of the year, so you should not hesitate to go on a winter's day during the week. It's a perfect way to chase the blues away and pick up your spirits! Of course, the golden rule is to get there as early as possible, because the magnificent spectacle available is so diverse that every minute of your time is precious and full of surprises.

Even queuing up at the entrance to an attraction can be entertaining, thanks to the decor evoking its theme and the street shows that help pass the time in a fun, relaxed atmosphere. Cast Members are there to organize the queues and inform visitors of expected waiting times.

As restaurants serve meals at all times of day, you can avoid crowds by eating at off-peak hours. You can always tide yourself over with a snack in the meantime.

Numerous opportunities will arise during your trip through the five lands of the Euro Disneyland Park, where Chariots Gourmands (see p. 50) and counter service offer a variety of appetizing snacks.

Don't hesitate to go into the shops during the course of your visit in order to choose items at a leisurely pace. We highly recommend not waiting until the last minute, when departing visitors are in the shops at the end of the day looking for souvenirs of their

---

Euro Disneyland Park Operating Hours

Operating hours vary, depending on the period and time of year you plan to go.

From mid-April to the end of October, the Park opens at 9 am and closes between 7 pm and midnight. From early November to mid-April, the Park is open from 10 am to 6 pm during the week and from 10 am to 7 pm on weekends. The Christmas season is an exception to the rule. The celebrating starts at the Euro Disney Resort in the middle of December and goes on until the beginning of January. During that period the Park sometimes opens at 9 am and stays open until 10 pm or midnight, depending on the day.

Operating hours also change during school holidays, long weekends, national holidays such as Easter and Ascension Thursday, and during the months of July and August, when the Park is open from 9 am to midnight.

As these hours are subject to change, we recommend making further inquiries when planning your trip. Call Guest Relations at (33-1) 64 74 30 00.

---

visit to the Euro Disney Resort. Take this opportunity to see an attraction you passed up because there were too many people waiting to get in.

Please note that it's best to contact the Euro Disney Resort in advance for information concerning operating hours (see above box), which may be subject to modification.

How to get there

The Euro Disney Resort, located 32 kilometres east of Paris on the outskirts of the greater Paris area, is within easy reach of the French capital's transportation network.

The site is easily accessible by the A4 motorway as well as the RER A train (Regional Express Network fast trains serving the Paris area), whose last stop is Marne-la-Vallée - Chessy. As of June 1994, a new TGV line will also serve this station.
Moreover, the Park is equidistant from Paris' two international airports, Roissy-Charles de Gaulle and Orly. Communications between the Park and the two airports are quite rapid both by car and RER.
A direct shuttle-bus service from both airports has also been set up for visitors to the Euro Disney Resort.
If you are staying in Paris, we highly recommend taking the RER as opposed to going by car, given the traffic jams that often block the major routes around Paris during rush hour. Indeed, it takes no more than 35 minutes on the RER to get from Paris to Marne-la-Vallée - Chessy, located very near the Main Entrance to the Theme Park, Disneyland Hotel and Festival Disney.
The Euro Disney Resort is designed for pedestrians, and on site a system of free shuttle buses makes it easy to get around. However, if the need should arise during your visit, you may take a taxi or rent a car from Europcar (see p. 49).

BY CAR

The French motorway network, with Paris at its hub, provides ideal access to the Euro Disney Resort. To get to the A4, we recommend taking the access roads linking the different motorways in order to avoid the city of Paris and its ring roads.
The simultaneous development of motorways in other European countries has vastly reduced driving time between capitals. Thus, the Euro Disney Resort is now only about a 6 ½ hour drive from London. There are several ways to get to the Euro Disney Resort from the United Kingdom and the Scandinavian countries. The following itineraries are the routes we've found to be the fastest and most direct.

From the United Kingdom. The most regular ferries crossing the Channel to Calais and Boulogne leave from Dover and Folkestone:
— Dover-Calais: 1 h 15 or 1 h 30 by ferry and 35 mins by hovercraft;
— Dover-Boulogne: 1 h 40 by ferry and 35 mins by hovercraft;
— Folkestone-Boulogne: 1 h 50 by ferry;
— Folkestone-Calais: 1 h 40 by ferry.
For maritime transportation, contact P&O European Ferries. Crossings are quite frequent and you can always board without prior reservations. The most direct routes to get to the Euro Disney Resort via Dover (69 kms southeast of London) and Folkestone

(61 kms southeast of London) converge at the M5 motorway that runs around the capital and heads southeast; from there, take the A20 to one of the two ports.
From Calais, take the A26, then the A1 towards Paris. After passing Roissy, we advise taking the A104, then the A4 all the way to the Euro Disney Resort.
From Boulogne, take the N42 to Saint-Omer, then the A26 towards Paris, then proceed as above.

From Ireland. It's possible to go directly from Ireland to France by ferry boat, from Rosslare to Le Havre. But you can also go through the United Kingdom. The Dublin-Holyhead crossing takes 3 h 30 and ferries run every day. From there, take the fast A5 to Birmingham, then the M1 and M25 motorways towards London and the A20 to Dover or Folkestone.

From Denmark. The fastest route goes through Hamburg, Germany. From there, take the motorway through Bremen, Hanover, Frankfurt, Mannheim and Sarrebruck to Metz, then take the A4 to the Euro Disney Resort. It's also possible to go from Bremen via Dusseldorf, Liège and Namur (in Belgium), then take the E19-A2 motorway and finally the A1 via Valenciennes. After passing Roissy, head east on the A104, then take the A4 to the Euro Disney Resort exit.

From the other Scandinavian countries. The quickest route from Norway, Sweden and Finland is through Hamburg, Germany, which can be reached by boat. The German ports of Kiel and Travemunde are located 150 and 60 kms respectively

---

Distances between the Euro Disney Resort and major cities in Northern Europe by car	
United Kingdom	
From Glasgow	940 kms
From London	465 kms
From Manchester	610 kms
Ireland	
From Dublin	710 kms
Denmark	
From Copenhagen	1,230 kms
Finland	
From Helsinki	2,290 kms
Norway	
From Oslo	1,810 kms
Sweden	
From Stockholm	1,850 kms

---

from Hamburg. From Hamburg, follow the routes indicated above.

Driving in France. All French motorways have tolls (payable with international credit cards), except in the Paris area. The Paris-Euro Disney Resort section of the motorway is free. Different grades of petrol are available at varying prices at all service stations, as well as mechanics' shops providing basic auto repairs. French driving regulations comply with those of other European countries with the following exceptions:
— The speed limit is 130 kms/hour on motorways, 110 kms/hour on double-

lane roads, 90 kms/hour on smaller roads and 50 kms/hour in towns and urban areas.

— In urban areas, the vehicle to your right has the right of way except at roundabouts indicating the contrary.

— The alcohol test allows a level of 0.80 g/l of alcohol in the blood.

Before leaving, don't forget your driving licence, car registration and international insurance policy.

For further information, contact the Automobile Club de l'Ile-de-France, 14, avenue de la Grande-Armée, 75017 Paris, tel.: (33-1) 43 80 68 58.

BY RER

Marne-la-Vallée - Chessy is now the last stop on the A train line of the RER (Regional Express Network) providing direct communications between the centre of Paris and the Euro Disney Resort. Parisian train stations are also linked up with the Park through the combined RER-metro network. All stops within the city of Paris on the A train line of the RER enable you to connect with the metro system. As a general rule, lines on the RER network have several destinations. For this reason, it's wise to check the signs suspended above platforms indicating whether the train in question is scheduled to stop at your destination. It takes about 35 minutes to get from Châtelet-Les Halles to Euro Disneyland Park.

With the RATP's yellow tickets you can travel by bus, metro and RER anywhere in Paris. Travelling on the RER outside of Paris requires buying a special ticket, whose price is based on your destination's distance from the city. The Euro Disney Resort is located in zone 5. Tickets can be bought in railway stations at "suburbs" ticket counters, as well as in metro and RER stations. For further information concerning the Parisian transportation system, ring the following number: (33-1) 43 46 14 14.

BY TRAIN

From the United Kingdom. British Rail (tel.: (071) 928 51 00) and SNCF run two trains in the daytime and one at night between London and Paris via Calais or Boulogne by train + boat or hovercraft (only during the day). The trip takes between 6 and 7 hours by day (the night trip is longer). The voyage can also be made via Dieppe. The Channel crossing is included in the price of your ticket, and a shuttle bus will transport you between stations and ferry boats.

A variety of discounts are available, depending on the length of your visit.

From Ireland. After taking the ferry boat from Dublin to Holyhead, in Wales, take the train to London. Then proceed to Paris as indicated above (minimum 19-hour trip).

From the Scandinavian countries.

There's one direct train per day that runs from Copenhagen to Paris-Nord in 16 hours. Two other trains run the same route, but they make stopovers. For further information, call D.S.B., tel.: 33 14 88 80.

There are no direct trains from Stockholm, so you must take a boat then catch the Paris train in Copenhagen or Hamburg (minimum 25-hour trip) For information, call S.J., tel.: (08) 22 79 40.

From Oslo, you also have to go through Copenhagen (minimum 25-

hour trip). For information, contact N.S.B., tel.: (02) 36 80 00.

From Helsinki, take a boat to Stockholm, then Copenhagen or Hamburg, where you can catch a train to Paris (minimum 39-hour trip).

If you intend to use the French railroad system (SNCF), the following two telephone numbers will be very useful:
— SNCF travel information: (33-1) 45 82 50 50;
— Reservations (for all stations): (33-1) 45 65 60 60, between 8 am and 8 pm.

You can also reserve train tickets through the minitel, an on-line telephone directory, by typing 3615 SNCF (available in France only.)

Fares vary according to the day of the week and time of year you travel. They are least expensive during the blue periods, standard during the white periods and most expensive during the red ones. Ask for more details when making your reservation.

The TGV already connects many cities in France with Paris. The Euro Disney Resort connection will be operational as of 1994.

TEE (Trans-Europ-Express) trains also run between Brussels (and sometimes as far as Antwerp), Luxemburg (via Reims or Metz) and Paris. For further information, contact the SNCB, Belgian railroad company, at the following numbers: in Belgium, (02) 648 41 01; in Luxemburg, 49 24 24.

The SNCF and other railroad companies offer numerous special fares for weekends, long trips, large families, people over 60 and under 26 years of age, and children. For further information concerning the special fares, contact the railroad companies at the above-mentioned telephone numbers.

Approximate travelling times by airplane between the Euro Disney Resort and major cities in Northern Europe, including trips between airports and the Resort

United Kingdom	
London	2 h 30
Ireland	
Dublin	3 h 10
Denmark	
Copenhagen	3 h 30
Finland	
Helsinki	4 h 30
Norway	
Oslo	3 h 30
Sweden	
Stockholm	4 h

Parisian train stations. Paris has six train stations, each one serving a different part of France and adjacent countries.

Trains from northern France and London (via Calais and Boulogne) as well as those from Scandinavian countries (via Copenhagen and Hamburg) arrive at the Gare du Nord in the 10th arrondissement. From Gare du Nord take RER Line B in the direction of Saint-Rémy-lès-Chevreuse to Châtelet-Les Halles, then catch the A train to Marne-la-Vallée - Chessy.

Trains from northwestern France and London (via Dieppe and Le Havre) arrive at the Gare Saint-Lazare in the 8th arrondissement. From Saint-Lazare to get to Line A, take metro Line n° 3 in the direction of Galliéni to Havre-Caumartin, where an underground passageway leads to Auber.

Trains coming from western France, as well as the TGV Atlantique from southwestern France, arrive at the Gare Montparnasse in the 14th arrondissement. From Montparnasse take metro Line n° 4 in the direction of Porte de Clignancourt to Les Halles, change and take Line A bound for Marne-la-Vallée - Chessy at Châtelet-Les Halles.

Trains coming from eastern France, Germany, Luxemburg and the Eastern European countries arrive at the Gare de l'Est in the 10th arrondissement. From the Gare de l'Est take Line n° 4 in the direction of Porte d'Orléans to Les Halles, where you can catch Line A (Châtelet-Les Halles station) to Marne-la-Vallée - Chessy.

TGV trains coming from southeastern France and Switzerland, as well as international trains from Italy, arrive at the Gare de Lyon in the 12th arrondissement, where you can take RER Line A to Marne-la-Vallée - Chessy .

Corail, overnight and international trains coming from southwestern France, Spain and Portugal arrive at the Gare d'Austerlitz in the 13th arrondissement. The one exception is the TGV Atlantique, which arrives at the Gare Montparnasse. To get to RER Line A from the Gare d'Austerlitz, take metro Line n° 5 heading in the direction of Bobigny-Pablo Picasso to Bastille. Change at Bastille by taking Line n° 1 in the direction of Château de Vincennes to the Gare de Lyon or Nation. From there, the Line A will

take you directly to Marne-la-Vallée - Chessy. The bus route is even simpler. The 24, 57, 65 and 91 buses all go straight to the Gare de Lyon, where you can catch the RER.

BY AIRPLANE

Once in France you can obtain information about your return flight through the minitel service. Type 3615 HORAV, or 36 25 05 05. A system of special fares is also offered, similar to the one used by the railroad companies. On blue flights the fares are very low; on white flights they're a bit higher, and on red flights you must pay the full fare. Ask for more detailed information when reserving your ticket.

Most European airlines fly into Roissy, including British Airways, Dan Air, Aer Lingus, S.A.S. and Finnair, as well as Air France flights arriving from points around Europe. However, certain flights do land at Orly. You'll be informed of the correct airport when reserving your ticket.

Whether you fly into Roissy-Charles de Gaulle or Orly, getting to the Euro Disney Resort will be quite easy. S.A.S. has flights from the Scandinavian countries (Denmark, Norway and Sweden) to Paris, and Finnair flies between Finland and Paris.

Roissy-Charles de Gaulle Airport. If you fly into this airport, you can take an airport shuttle bus directly to the Euro Disney Resort from all air terminals. It leaves every half hour. Getting to the Euro Disney Resort on the RER is also very fast. First, take the free shuttle bus to the RER station at Roissy. From there, Roissy Rail (RER Line B in the direction of Saint-Rémy-lès-Chevreuse) takes you to

Châtelet-Les Halles where you can catch Line A to Marne-la-Vallée - Chessy. The airport, like the Euro Disney Resort, is located in fare zone 5. If you're going by car, take the A1 in the direction of Paris, then get on the A104 in the direction of Marne-la-Vallée - Chessy. After that, take the A4 in the direction of Metz until you reach the Euro Disney Resort. Call (33-1) 48 62 22 80 for information.

Orly airport. If you fly into this airport, you can take an airport shuttle bus (leaving every 45 min) directly to the Euro Disney Resort.

The trip from Orly to the Euro Disney Resort on the RER is now quite fast thanks to the new Orlyval service that takes you directly to the station in Antony. From there, take RER Line B in the direction of Mitry-Claye-Roissy to Châtelet-Les Halles, change and take Line A directly to Marne-la-Vallée - Chessy.

If you go by car, take the A86 to get on to the A4, which leads you directly to the Euro Disney Resort.

Call (33-1) 49 75 15 15 for information.

BY TAXI

Taxis are available for travellers at airports, train stations and in front of all metro and RER stations. They can also be hailed in the street. Taxis are only authorized to take three passengers, except for the larger Renault Espace models which can take up to six people. Taxi fares to the Euro Disney Resort range from about 250 F from Paris to 300 F from the airports. Below is a list of telephone numbers for the major Parisian taxicab companies. The lines are often busy, so be patient!

G7 Radio	47 39 47 39
Taxis Bleus	49 36 10 10
Taxi Radio Étoile	42 70 41 41

Airline companies

AIR FRANCE
119, av. des Champs-Élysées
75008 Paris.
Tel.: (33-1) 45 35 61 61.
158, New Bond Street, London.
Tel.: (071) 499 95 11.
Dawson House, 29/30
Dawson Street, Dublin.
Tel.: 77 88 99.
Vesterbrogade 1A, København.
Tel.: 33 12 76 76.
Fridtjof Nansens Plass 6, Oslo.
Tel.: (02) 42 10 45.
Norrlandsgatan 7, Stockholm.
Tel.: (08) 23 42 00.
Pohjoisesplanadi 27 C, Helsinki.
Tel.: (90) 62 58 62.

BRITISH AIRWAYS
12, rue de Castiglione 75001 Paris.
Tel.: (33-1) 47 78 14 14.
Heathrow Airport London
PO Box 10 - Hounslow TW6 2JA.
Tel.: (081) 759 55 11.

DAN AIR
31, rue du Pont
92200 Neuilly-sur-Seine.
Tel.: (33-1) 47 47 44 44.
Nowman House, Victoria
House - Horley, Sussex, RH8 7QG.
Tel.: (0293) 820 700.

AER LINGUS
47, av. de l'Opéra 75002 Paris.
Tel.: (33-1) 47 42 12 50.
Dublin Airport, Dublin.
Tel.: (01) 37 00 11.

S.A.S.
30, bd des Capucines 75009 Paris.
Tel.: (33-1) 47 42 06 14.
Building Hammerichsgade,
København.
Tel.: 33 13 72 77.
Stenersgt 1A, Oslo.
Tel.: (02) 59 62 40.
Froesundaviks Alle 1, Stockholm.
Tel.: (08) 79 70 00.

FINNAIR
11, rue Auber 75009 Paris.
Tel.: (33-1) 47 42 33 33.
Mannerheimintie 102, Helsinki.
Tel.: (90) 81 88 00.

Arriving at the
Euro Disney Resort

No matter what the means of transportation used to get there, guests realize as soon as they arrive at the Euro Disney Resort that they're now in a land made for pedestrians! If they've come in their own car, they may go directly to the Park and leave the car in the nearby Guest Parking (see p. 48). If they prefer, they may stop at their hotel or campground first, where parking is also available, and then proceed onwards to the Park or Festival Disney. The Gare Routière (bus Station) near the RER and future TGV station, is where shuttle buses and taxis arrive, as well as cars with passengers to drop off (see p. 49). A free shuttle-bus system runs inside the Euro Disney Resort. Two lines connect the hotels situated around the lake or on the banks of the Rio Grande with the Theme Park and Festival Disney, and a third line links the campground and golf course to the Theme Park and Festival Disney (see p. 49).

BY CAR

If you've reserved a cabin trailer or tent/caravan space in the Camp Davy Crockett, leave the A4 at the Provins exit and follow the signs to the reception office in the campground "village" (see p. 145). From there, a free shuttle bus will take you to the Theme Park or Festival Disney (see p. 49).

However, if you're staying at one of the six Euro Disney Resort hotels, take the Euro Disney Resort exit and follow the signs to your hotel. You can leave your car in the car park for the duration of your stay and use the shuttle buses that will take you to the Theme Park or Festival Disney (see p. 49).

If you prefer to go directly to the Park or Festival Disney, take the Euro Disney Resort exit and follow the signs to Guest Parking which has 9,000 spaces. Count on paying 30 F for a car, 20 F for a motorcycle, and 50 F for a caravan or camping car. A special car park for handicapped guests is located near the Park entrance (see p. 45). The Esplanade equipped with covered moving sidewalks allows you to go directly from Guest Parking to the Main Entrance of Euro Disneyland Park (see p. 33).

You may leave your car in Guest Parking during the day, but vehicles are not allowed to stay there overnight. So, if you plan on staying at one of the hotels or at the campground, don't forget to put your car in the car parks provided there.

BY TAXI

If you arrive by taxi and want to go directly to your hotel or to the campground, follow the same procedure as someone arriving by car (see above).

You can use the free shuttle buses to get around inside the Euro Disney Resort (see p. 49).

To go directly to the Theme Park or Festival Disney, get off at the Gare Routière near the Main Entrance to the Park.

BY RER

The RER station (Marne-la-Vallée - Chessy) is located in front of the entrance to the Park, just next to Festival Disney. You can walk to either location in no time at all.

Guest Storage, where you can leave large packages, is available at the entrance to the Park.

If you want to go to your hotel room or cabin first, take one of the free shuttle buses that run inside the Euro Disney Resort.

Getting into the Park

All visitors first gather at Disney Square, near the RER station, the bus stop and the moving sidewalks connected to the parking lot. From there, you can walk to the Disneyland Hotel where the entrance to the Euro Disneyland Park is located. In front of the hotel, flowerbeds and trees surround an ornamental pool full of fountains. You will be greeted by a floral Mickey Mouse and friendly Euro Disneyland Cast Members.

Ticket booths. Numerous, attractive ticket booths are to be found on the ground floor of the Disneyland Hotel. Guests can buy tickets for the Park, called Passports, and also exchange foreign currencies there. A special booth exists for groups. You can also buy the tickets at your Euro Disney Resort hotel or at Camp Davy Crockett.

The Euro Disneyland Passport gives you unlimited access to all attractions in the Park, with the exception of the Rustler Roundup Shootin' Gallery (see p. 72) in Frontierland. Passports are on sale at the Park's Main Entrance on the ground floor of the Disneyland Hotel, at Camp Davy Crockett and in the other Euro Disney Resort hotels. Children under the age of 7 must be accompanied by an adult, and children under the age of 2 are admitted free. There are two different admission fees for the Park, one for children between the ages of 3 and 11 and another for guests starting at age 12. It's also possible to buy a Multiday Passport, valid for two or three consecutive days or any other day in the future. For all information call (33 - 1) 64 74 30 00.

Buying Passports

By mail you can write to:
Euro Disney S.C.A.
Service Tickets
BP 103
F-77777 Marne-la-Vallée, Cedex 4, France.
By telephone you can call the following number:
(33-1) 64 74 43 03

Payment. There are several ways of paying for your Passport: either with cash (French and foreign currencies), a personal cheque in French francs, a Eurocheque, French francs traveller's cheques or with a credit card (Carte Bleue, Visa, Eurocard or Mastercard). American Express credit cards and traveller's cheques are also accepted.

Tickets for Guided Tours of the Park are available at the ticket booths situated at the Main Entrance. This walking tour is the perfect way to satisfy the curiosity of the guest who wants to learn more about Walt Disney, The Walt Disney Company and the Euro Disneyland Park. If that description fits you, then see you at The Arboretum on Town Square, Main Street, U.S.A. (see p. 58)! Foreign-language tours are also offered.

Some practical information to make your stay more pleasant:

— If you want to leave the Park and come back later on in the same day, don't forget to get your hand stamped with a magic invisible ink stamp at the exit. All you have to do to get back in is show your hand stamp and your Passport at the re-entry turnstile.

— At Guest Storage, located outside the Park, guests can leave large parcels. Inside the Park, use the coin-operated lockers located underneath Main Street Station.

— Located on either side of the Main Entrance, Plaza West and Plaza East Boutiques sell all sorts of useful things you might need during your visit — film, rainwear, sunglasses, hats and sun-care products (in the summer season), plus souvenirs, T-shirts and postcards.

— Passport in hand, you walk through the turnstiles. At last you are inside the magical world of the Euro Disneyland Park. High up in front of you is the outline of Main Street Station. This is where Main Street, U.S.A., the first land in the Park, begins. In the background you can make out the enchanting silhouette of Le Château de la Belle au Bois Dormant in Fantasyland.

Your Euro Disney Resort holiday

The Euro Disney Resort is far more than a mere amusement park in which to spend a few hours. It's a complete holiday experience in its own right.

A MULTIFACETED RESORT

The abundant and diverse forms of entertainment offered at the Euro Disney Resort make it a unique place to visit for people of all tastes, ages, and lifestyles.

The choice of entertainment is huge. First, there is Euro Disneyland Park, the Theme Park with magical attractions and shows so numerous that you can't fit them all into one day. Then there's the Festival Disney entertainment centre, which has a number of typical American restaurants, a discotheque and a spectacular dinner show about the Wild West. Festival Disney, which stays open until very late, is located next to the Main Entrance to the Park. There is also a campground, themed hotels and recreational facilities that will guarantee you a change of scenery and fun-filled holidays in ideal surroundings.

"Making families feel welcome and satisfying everyone's needs" could very well be the Euro Disney Resort motto. Everything has been arranged so that children and adults can have fun together. It's also possible to split up and let each person pursue the activities he or she finds most interesting. Afterwards, the whole group can meet back at their hotel room or at the campground to share their experiences of the day.

Visiting the surrounding area while staying at the Euro Disney Resort is an appealing idea for a great many visitors. In addition to Paris, whose charms are legendary, Ile-de-France possesses a wealth of famous sites such as Versailles, Fontainebleau and Vaux-le-Vicomte. Contact Guest Services about Euro Disney Resort excursion buses that will take you there. They also offer trips to the Champagne region, including a visit to the famous city of Reims.

Mixing business with pleasure is only natural at the Euro Disney Resort, where the huge New York Coliseum Convention Center, located in the Hotel New York complex, is equipped to host conventions, seminars, conferences and meetings of all kinds. This impressive, 2,300 m^2 conference centre can hold up to 2,000 people. Composed of a variety of different spaces, the largest of which is divisible into twelve separate rooms, it can accommodate everything from small receptions to large congresses. The Newport Bay Club and the Sequoia Lodge also have reception rooms. Theme parties, shows and various kinds of entertainment, including a wide variety of services, can be arranged.

To reserve, contact:
Euro Disney S.C.A.
Ventes, groupes et congrès
BP 100
F-77777 Marne-la-Vallée Cedex 4, France.
Tel.: (1) 49 32 46 73
Fax: (1) 49 32 46 62

PLANNING YOUR HOLIDAY

Visitors to the Euro Disney Resort will inevitably have to make choices based on the length of their stay and their individual preferences. The best way to experience all the excitement is to plan an extended stay with Euro Disney Resort as your holiday base.

If you decide to spend several days at the Euro Disney Resort, either at one of the hotels or at the campground, you can buy a package directly through the Euro Disney Resort or your local travel agent. By booking a Euro Disney package at one of the Resort hotels, you will receive exclusive benefits including the "Length of Stay Passport", which guarantees your admission to Euro Disneyland Park from the minute you arrive to the end of the day of your departure. You'll also enjoy early admission to Euro Disneyland Park during peak season, plus free transportation to all areas of the Resort. It's also possible to buy a Multiday Passport at our Guest Services desks at the hotels or the ticket booths at the Main Entrance to Euro Disneyland Park. That way, you're free to come and go as you please for several days of fun inside the Park.

If you only have one day, you'll probably spend most of your time in the Theme Park. Allow us to give you a few tips that will help you get the most out of your visit to the extraordinary world of Euro Disneyland Park. Try to arrive early, at least half an hour before the Theme Park opens, so you can get into the Park as quickly as possible. Take your meals outside of regular hours (the French eat lunch at strict times, between noon and 2 pm). Light refreshments will help tide you over.

Avoid shopping at the end of the day. Try to go to the shops when they are less crowded, for instance at meal times. Don't miss the ones in Main Street, U.S.A. that you can reach through a worthwhile detour in the Liberty and Discovery Arcades. And don't forget the shops in the hotels and Festival Disney. Get the most out of your day — remember that attractions are open until closing time. Take these general guidelines into account when planning your day's activities, but above all let your imagination be your guide. For starters, how about meeting some famous Walt Disney characters at a Character Breakfast at either the Disneyland Hotel or Hotel New York (see pps. 123 and 126)?

Inside the Park, stroll around at your leisure, but be sure not to miss attractions like Big Thunder Mountain, Phantom Manor, and the boat rides in Frontierland; Adventure Isle and Pirates of the Caribbean in Adventureland; Le Château de la Belle au Bois Dormant, Le Théâtre du Château and It's a Small World in Fantasyland; Star Tours, Ciné-Magique and Le Visionarium in Discoveryland.

And that's not all! Outdoor shows and street entertainment are going on all the time in the various lands, not to mention the parade that winds through the streets of Fantasyland and Main Street, U.S.A. as well as Main Street Electrical Parade and fireworks that will brighten many an evening.

There are also themed restaurants, dinner shows and discotheques in the Park, such as The Lucky Nugget Saloon in Frontierland; Blue Lagoon Restaurant in Adventureland; Videopolis in Discoveryland. In Festival Disney, enjoy The Steakhouse, Billy Bob's Country Western Saloon, Hurricanes and above all the spectacular Buffalo Bill's Wild West Show, a dinner show, complete with real Wild West animals. You'll love it after a day full of fun!

The shops at Euro Disneyland Park are anything but ordinary. In Adventureland, you'll find yourself strolling through an exotic bazaar, whereas in Discoveryland you can do your shopping on board a spaceship.

ACCOMMODATION

The Euro Disney Resort includes a campground and six hotels situated on Lake Buena Vista or along the Rio Grande, with the exception of the Disneyland Hotel which overlooks the entrance to the Euro Disneyland Park. Each one is an attraction unto itself, with its own theme that is echoed throughout its shops, restaurants, decor and Cast Members in costume.

Hotels. Each hotel has its own guest information desk where you can obtain information about other hotels in the Euro Disney Resort, buy Passports for the Park, make reservations for Resort restaurants and shows, rent a car, etc... All rooms are designed for families of four.

The Disneyland Hotel, a luxury-class establishment, was designed in the style of a turn-of-the-century Victorian hotel. Located at the entrance to the Theme Park, it offers a spectacular panoramic view of Main Street and Le Château de la Belle au Bois Dormant.

Hotel New York re-creates the atmosphere of Manhattan, in the heart of that great American metropolis, with a eight-storey skyscraper, an evocation of Central Park and an open-air skating rink.

The Newport Bay Club is designed in the style of a New England seaside resort hotel at the turn of the century, including a veranda decorated with rocking chairs and a lakeside boardwalk leading to a lighthouse.

The Sequoia Lodge, located in a wooded area by the lake between two inlet rivers, is reminiscent of the rustic lodges found in the American National Parks. In the winter, a huge fireplace in the lounge adds to the feeling of cosy comfort.

Hotel Cheyenne is built in the style of a frontier town in the Far West, surrounded by a landscape right out of a Hollywood western, complete with wooden fort and Indian teepees.

Hotel Santa Fe, designed in the style of a Pueblo Indian village, brings to mind the desert landscapes of New Mexico in the American Southwest.

The Campground. In the heart of a hundred-year-old forest, Camp Davy Crockett evokes the era of American fur traders. You can pitch your tent or park your caravan car there. You may also stay in one of the comfortably appointed log cabins for four to six people.

"All-inclusive" Holidays. The hotels and campground offer various two- or three-day "all-inclusive" holidays ranging in style from "campground comfort" to "moderate", "first class", and "luxury".

Packages include the price of your room with breakfast at one of the hotels or at the campground, unlimited access to the Park and free use of the Euro Disney shuttles. Some even include excursions to famous sights throughout Ile-de-France. A variety of other advantages, such as access to various sports and fitness

---

Reservations

To reserve a room or cabin, call one of the following telephone numbers:
From United Kingdom
071-753 2900 (in London)
From Ireland
(33-1) 49 41 49 10
From Denmark
(33-1) 49 41 49 20
From Finland
(33-1) 49 41 49 75
From Norway
(33-1) 49 41 49 50
From Sweden
(33-1) 49 41 49 70
You can also reserve by fax:
(33-1) 49 30 71 00 or 49 30 71 70
by telex:
232 642 or 232 647
or by mail:
Euro Disney S.C.A., Central Reservations, BP 105, F-77777 Marne-la-Vallée Cedex 4, France.
The office is open seven days a week from 8 am to 8 pm.

A deposit confirming your reservation is required; however, this deposit is fully refunded if you cancel your reservation within five days of the appointed date.

---

activities, dinner or tickets for Buffalo Bill's Wild West Show, are also offered depending on which all-inclusive holiday you choose.

SPORTS AND LEISURE ACTIVITIES

During your stay, you'll want to get the most out of your leisure time by participating in the numerous activities available at the Euro Disney Resort.

The following are some of the **sports and fitness activities** available for Resort guests:
— Health clubs with gym, sauna and whirlpool at the Disneyland Hotel,

Hotel New York, the Newport Bay Club and the Sequoia Lodge.
— Indoor and outdoor swimming pools at the Sequoia Lodge, the Newport Bay Club, Hotel New York, the Disneyland Hotel and Camp Davy Crockett.
— Tennis courts at Hotel New York and Camp Davy Crockett.
— A jogging track around Lake Buena Vista and in the campground.
— A fabulous 18-hole golf course with lakes, large bunkers and waterfalls (open as of autumn 1992). The golf course, although designed to host professional tournaments, is nevertheless an ideal place for all golfers.
— A fitness trail at Camp Davy Crockett.
Other activities available for visitors:
— Croquet at the Newport Bay Club.
— Bike rental and pony rides at Camp Davy Crockett.
— Boat rental in front of The Steakhouse in Festival Disney.
— Ice skating in wintertime at Rockefeller Plaza in front of Hotel New York.
During the winter season, it's time to sharpen your skates and head for the skating rink, where you'll feel as if you were right in the heart of New York City.
The rink is open from 10 am to 10 pm. Admission prices for two hours of skating range from 40 F for adults (50 F with skates) to 30 F for groups.

Disneyland Hotel (Luxury-Class Hotel)

500 rooms including 21 suites and 11 rooms for the handicapped. Non-smoking rooms available. Check-in from 3 pm. Check-out by 11 am.

	Peak Season	Mid Season	Off Season
DATES	• mid-April to end of October • mid-December to early January	• weekends (Friday and Saturday night) • from early November to mid-April (except Christmas holidays)	• early November to mid-April (except weekends and Christmas holidays)
RATES per night	• from 1,950 FF per room • from 4,050 FF per suite	• from 1,600 FF per room • from 3,350 FF per suite	• from 1,300 FF per room • from 2,700 FF per suite

All room rates are valid up to a family of four.

• Health Club: exercise machines, aerobics, massage, solarium equipment, sauna, steam room, whirlpool, and health-food snack bar • Indoor heated swimming pool • Rooms equipped with colour television featuring cable, closed-circuit programmes and international channels; mini-bar; air conditioning • Castle Club: private access and special services on certain floors • Game Rooms • Laundry and Dry-Cleaning Service • Baby-sitting service in room • Dining: California Grill, Inventions, Café Fantasia and Main Street Lounge • Galerie Mickey (Disney Shop).

Hotel New York (Luxury/Convention-Class Hotel)

574 rooms including 36 suites and 13 rooms for the handicapped. Non-smoking rooms available. Check-in from 3 pm. Check-out by 11 am.

	Peak Season	Mid Season	Off Season
DATES	• mid-April to end of October • mid-December to early January	• weekends (Friday and Saturday night) • from early November to mid-April (except Christmas holidays)	• early November to mid-April (except weekends and Christmas holidays)
RATES per night	• from 1,600 FF per room • from 2,400 FF per suite	• from 1,350 FF per room • from 2,000 FF per suite	• from 1,100 FF per room • from 1,600 FF per suite

All room rates are valid up to a family of four.

• Health Club : exercise machines, aerobics, massage, solarium equipment, sauna, steam room, whirlpool, and health-food snack bar • Indoor and outdoor heated swimming pools • Open-air skating rink (in wintertime) • Two tennis courts with night lighting • Rooms equipped with colour television featuring cable, closed-circuit programmes and international channels; mini-bar; air conditioning; minitel (on-line telephone directory) and Videotex • Castle Club: private access and special services on certain floors • Game Rooms • Laundry and Dry-Cleaning Service • Beauty Salon/Barber shop • Baby-sitting service in room • Dining: Rainbow Room, Rainbow Lounge, Parkside Diner, 57th Street Bar • Convention Centre • Stock Exchange (Disney Shop) • Free transportation to the Theme Park.

Newport Bay Club (First-Class Hotel)

1,098 rooms including 15 suites and 23 rooms for the handicapped. Non-smoking rooms available. Check-in from 3 pm. Check-out by 11 am.

	Peak Season	Mid Season	Off Season
DATES	• mid-April to end of October • mid-December to early January	• weekends (Friday and Saturday night) • from early November to mid-April (except Christmas holidays)	• early November to mid-April (except weekends and Christmas holidays)
RATES per night	• from 1,110 FF per room • from 1,700 FF per suite	• from 950 FF per room • from 1,400 FF per suite	• from 750 FF per room • from 1,150 FF per suite

All room rates are valid up to a family of four.

• Health Club: exercise machines, aerobics, steam room, sauna, solarium equipment, massage and whirlpool • Indoor swimming pool with snack bar; outdoor pool with solarium • Rooms equipped with colour television featuring cable, closed-circuit programmes and international channels; mini-bar; air conditioning • Game Rooms • Croquet Field • Children's playground • Baby-sitting service in room • Laundry and Dry-Cleaning Service • Dining: Yacht Club, Cape Cod, Fisherman's Wharf • Convention/Reception Rooms • Bay Boutique (Disney Shop) • Free transportation to the Theme Park.

40

Sequoia Lodge (First-Class Hotel)

1,011 rooms including 14 suites and 21 rooms for the handicapped. Non-smoking rooms available. Check-in from 3 pm. Check-out by 11 am.

	Peak Season	Mid Season	Off Season
DATES	• mid-April to end of October • mid-December to early January	• weekends (Friday and Saturday night) • from early November to mid-April (except Christmas holidays)	• early November to mid-April (except weekends and Christmas holidays)
RATES per night	• from 1,100 FF per room • from 1,700 FF per suite	• from 950 FF per room • from 1,400 FF per suite	• from 750 FF per room • from 1,150 FF per suite

All room rates are valid up to a family of four.

• Health Club: exercise machines, aerobics, whirlpool, massage, sauna, solarium equipment and steam room • Indoor and outdoor swimming pools with slides, cascades and health-food snack bar • Rooms equipped with colour television featuring cable, closed-circuit programmes and international channels; mini-bar; air conditioning • Game Rooms • Children's playground • Laundry and Dry-Cleaning Service • Dining: Hunter's Grill, Beaver Creek Tavern, Redwood Bar and Lounge • Convention/Reception Rooms • North West Passage (Disney Shop) • Free transportation to the Theme Park.

Hotel Cheyenne (Moderate Class Hotel)

1,000 rooms, including 21 for the handicapped, located in 14 frontier-style buildings. Bunkbeds for children and non-smoking rooms available. Check-in from 3 pm. Check-out by 11 am.

	Peak Season	Mid Season	Off Season
DATES	• mid-April to end of October • mid-December to early January	• weekends (Friday and Saturday night) • from early November to mid-April (except Christmas holidays)	• early November to mid-April (except weekends and Christmas holidays)
RATES per night	• 750 FF per room	• 650 FF per room	• 550 FF per room

All room rates are valid up to a family of four.

• Rooms equipped with colour television featuring cable, closed-circuit programmes and international channels; mini-bar • Game Rooms • Laundry and Dry-Cleaning Service • Children's playground • Baby-sitting service in room • Dining: Chuckwagon Cafe, Red Garter Saloon • General Store (Disney Shop) • Free transportation to the Theme Park.

Hotel Santa Fe (Moderate-Class Hotel)

1,000 rooms, including 21 for the handicapped, located in 42 Pueblo-style buildings. Non-smoking rooms available. Check-in from 3 pm. Check-out by 11 am.

	Peak Season	Mid Season	Off Season
DATES	• mid-April to end of October • mid-December to early January	• weekends (Friday and Saturday night) • from early November to mid-April (except Christmas holidays)	• early November to mid-April (except weekends and Christmas holidays)
RATES per night	• 750 FF per room	• 650 FF per room	• 550 FF per room

All room rates are valid up to a family of four.

• Rooms equipped with colour television featuring cable, closed-circuit programmes and international channels; mini-bar • Game Rooms • Children's playground • Baby-sitting service in room • Laundry and Dry-Cleaning Service • Dining: La Cantina, Rio Grande Bar • Trading Post (Disney Shop) • Free transportation to the Theme Park.

Camp Davy Crockett

181 campsites and 414 cabins accommodating between four and six people. Non-smoking cabins available. Check-in from 3 pm. Check-out by 11 am.

	Peak Season	Mid Season	Off Season
DATES	• mid-April to end of October • mid-December to early January	• weekends (Friday and Saturday night) • from early November to mid-April (except Christmas holidays)	• early November to mid-April (except weekends and Christmas holidays)
RATES per night	• 875 FF per cabin • 270 FF per campsite	• 725 FF per cabin • 270 FF per campsite	• 575 FF per cabin • 270 FF per campsite

Most cabin rates are valid up to a family of six.

• Cabins with bath, colour television featuring cable and international channels, telephone, heating, and daily housekeeping service • Comfort stations with shower, rest rooms, Laundromat, changing tables, and vending machines in campsite area • Indoor swimming pool with slides, river, whirlpool, kiddy pool, waterfall and health-food snack bar • Outdoor tennis courts • Sports fields (basketball, football, volleyball, pétanque) • Game Rooms • Campfires • Children's farm with pony rides • Bicycle and minicar rentals • Nature, bicycle and jogging trails • Dining: Crockett's Tavern • Alamo Trading Post (Disney Shop) • Free transportation to the Theme Park.

Life at the

Euro Disney Resort

THE LOCALS

The Characters. There they are! Mickey, Minnie, Pinocchio, Alice and many more of your storybook friends... greeting children and adults alike, posing for photos or playfully visiting your breakfast table. They're all here, the characters whose gaiety, spontaneity and eternal youthfulness have brought memorable smiles and laughter to their millions of fans.

Some of the most popular characters created by Walt Disney include Mickey, Minnie, Donald, Daisy, Goofy, Pluto, Chip an' Dale. Each with his or her own special personality, they are often found at the entrance to the Park happily greeting arriving guests.

Without a doubt, Mickey Mouse is the leader of this great gang of pals. Mickey, whose screen debut goes back to 1928, is full of wonderful qualities.

Intelligent, thoughtful, and a friend to everyone, Mickey is optimistic to the point of it being contagious, and disarmingly modest. The life of the party, he has a way of getting people going... and leading them into a whirlwind of comical adventures.

Mickey's sweetheart, Minnie Mouse, loves to tease him, even though she obviously adores him. Always the perfect lady, Minnie possesses great poise, as well as being a talented singer and dancer.

Donald Duck, best known for his lack of patience, is easily frustrated and gets upset when things don't go his way. Hidden underneath his boisterous antics lies a heart of gold which endears him to all he meets.

His sweetheart, Daisy, is delightfully feminine and flirtatious, which of course adds to Donald's dilemmas!

Lovable Goofy is forever bumbling his way through outrageous situations with a good-natured laugh! Goofy is a true sportsman, always giving his best.

Pluto is Mickey's loyal and affectionate canine companion. A good-natured puppy at heart, Pluto loves to play and is content when he is around people.

Chip an' Dale are the twin chipmunks whose boundless energy and hilarious mischievousness make them the perfect comedy team.

Once inside the Park, you'll meet many other Disney characters who

seem to have stepped directly from the tales and legends of European folklore. In Fantasyland, you'll delight in finding characters such as Snow White, Sleeping Beauty, Cinderella, Pinocchio, Robin Hood, Winnie the Pooh and, of course, Alice endlessly searching for her White Rabbit in Alice's Curious Labyrinth.

In Adventureland, Peter Pan continues to spar with his fierce enemy, Captain Hook, while poor Mr. Smee becomes even more frantic. The *Jungle Book* characters Mowgli, King Louie and Baloo have a rollicking good time roaming through the Adventureland Bazar.

In Discoveryland, you'll meet characters from the exciting world of science fiction! Chewbaka, the Ewoks and C3PO from *Star Wars* to name a few.

Of course, the sparkling Parade on Main Street provides a wonderful opportunity to see most of your favourite characters.

Outside the Park, Camp Davy Crockett is where you're most likely to find Chip an' Dale "cooking up a storm" around the campfire.

In the hotel area, Disney characters invite you to join them each morning for a Character Breakfast at Inventions in the Disneyland Hotel or at the Rainbow Room in Hotel New York (see box p. 38).

The Cast Members. Whatever their part may be, they're all members of the cast in the great, ongoing show at the Euro Disney Resort. Their role is to insure that guests have as pleasant a holiday as possible. They can handle any situation that arises and will answer any questions you may have about attractions, restaurants and other matters kindly and courteously. Most Cast Members are bilingual in French and English. Some of them also speak a third language, such as German, Dutch, Italian or Spanish.

GUESTS

Everything has been designed so that everyone can have a good time at the Euro Disney Resort, and absolutely everyone is welcome there, from tiny children to the elderly. Special facilities have been set up for children and the handicapped, and non-smoking areas have been designated.

There are no limits to the fun you can have. However, certain attractions — such as Big Thunder Mountain, Star Tours and Autopia — are not recommended for people with back or heart trouble, pregnant women and young children.

As for local Disney customs, here are a few guidelines to follow:

— proper dress is required; shirts (or tee-shirts) and shoes must be worn at all times;

— smoking is forbidden inside attractions and in waiting areas;

— eating, drinking, using video cameras, and taking photographs with a flash are not permitted inside the attractions;

— animals, except for Guide dogs, are not allowed inside the Park.

Children. They are naturally the guests of honour in the magical world of Walt Disney.

A Baby Care Center, hosted by Nestlé, located near Plaza Gardens Restaurant on Main Street, offers facilities for changing nappies and warming baby bottles. For safety reasons, very young children are not allowed to ride certain attractions. Orbitron, Dumbo the Flying Elephant and Autopia do not accept children under one year of age. Big Thunder Mountain and Autopia have a minimum height requirement.

You can rent a stroller (push chair) by the day at Town Square near the Main Entrance. Rental is 30 F per day with an additional 20 F refundable deposit when the stroller is returned. If you want, you may also bring your own stroller to the Park.

If your child gets lost, there's no need to worry. Children are immediately taken in hand by one of the Cast Members and taken to the Baby Care Center located near Plaza Gardens Restaurant in Main Street, U.S.A., where they are looked after until you come and get them. You may also inquire at the information office at City Hall on Town Square or ask any Cast Member for assistance.

In Festival Disney, the Never Land Club Children's Theater is a game room with a Peter Pan theme designed for children between the ages of three and ten. It is open from 5 pm until late in the evening. The children will have fun for several hours, while their parents enjoy the nightlife at the Euro Disney Resort (see p. 113).

In the Euro Disney hotels and campground, baby-sitting service is available. For additional details, inquire on site.

Handicapped Guests. At the Euro Disney Resort, everything has been designed to facilitate their visit:

— Parking spaces reserved for the handicapped visiting the Park are located near the Disneyland Hotel.

— Upon request, a special vehicle is provided for handicapped guests to get from the hotels or campground to the Theme Park.

— Hotels have specially equipped rooms for handicapped guests.

• For people in wheelchairs:

— Wheelchairs can be rented by the day at Town Square near the Main Entrance. Rental is 30 F per day with an additional 20 F refundable deposit when the wheelchair is returned.

— Special access to attractions, restaurants and shops in the Park is detailed in the Guest Special Services Guide available at the Main Entrance, City Hall and information booths throughout the Park.

— Spaces have been reserved for the handicapped at specific spots along the parade route, as well as at show sites. Cast Members at City Hall will provide you with the necessary information or assistance.

— Toilets are accessible by wheelchair. Those who require special help can inquire at First Aid, located near Plaza Gardens Restaurant.

— Telephones have been designed so that they can be used by people in wheelchairs.

— All restaurants and shops are accessible by wheelchair. Some shops are also equipped with special dressing rooms designed for the handicapped.

• For the blind or visually impaired:
— Guide dogs are allowed inside the Park. However, some attractions cannot accommodate the dogs.
— Portable headsets with audio cassettes are available for the visually impaired at City Hall in Main Street, U.S.A.

• A special telecommunications device is available for the hearing impaired at City Hall.

For more information or special assistance, inquire at City Hall on Main Street, U.S.A.

Foreign Guests. To enter France, visitors will be required to present a valid passport or identity card. Those with cars must have the vehicle's registration with them as well as an international insurance card delivered in the country of origin.

A wealth of information concerning tourism in the surrounding area is available at the Ile-de-France Maison du Tourisme in Festival Disney. Take the passageway leading to the mezzanine where the various services are located, including an exhibit on the history of the Ile-de-France region (see p. 114).

Consulate addresses:
— British Consulate/ 35, rue du Faubourg-St.-Honoré, 75008 Paris, tel.: (33-1) 42 66 91 42;
— Irish Consulate/ 4, rue Rude, 75016 Paris, tel.: (33-1) 45 00 20 87;
— Danish Consulate/ 77, avenue Marceau, 75016 Paris, tel.: (33-1) 44 31 21 21;
— Finnish Consulate/ 18 bis, rue d'Anjou, 75008 Paris, tel.: (33-1) 42 65 33 65;
— Swedish Consulate/ Section Consulaire, 17, rue Barbet de Jouy, 75007 Paris, tel.: (33-1) 45 55 92 15;
— Norwegian Consulate/ 28, rue Bayard, 75008 Paris, tel.: (33-1) 47 23 72 78.

LANGUAGES

French and English are the two official languages at the Euro Disney Resort, and they are the languages used in the shows. However, as the visual element in the shows is so important, everyone will be able to enjoy him or herself, no matter what his or her linguistic abilities.
Five languages (French, English, German, Spanish and Italian) are spoken at hotel and campground reception desks.

MONEY

Exchange. Guests may exchange foreign currencies at the Main Entrance to Euro Disneyland Park, at information booths located in the Park, as well as in Festival Disney, at the hotels and campground.

Cash withdrawals. BNP automatic cash dispensers accepting most international and French credit cards are located in Liberty and Discovery

Arcades in Main Street, U.S.A., in the Park (see p. 60).

There is also a cash distributor in the post office at Festival Disney (see p. 112).

Means of payment. Most restaurants and shops in the Euro Disney Resort accept major credit cards, Eurocheques, traveller's cheques in French francs as well as personal cheques in French francs with valid identification.

COMMUNICATIONS

The Post Office. A post office, run by French government postal employees with the Disney spirit of service, is located in Festival Disney.

Stamps are also available at The Storybook Store located on Town Square in Main Street, U.S.A. Letter boxes that blend in with the decor are located throughout the Park, the hotels and the campground.

Telephone. You'll find France Télécom booths with coin and card telephones in each land of the Euro Disneyland Park, in Festival Disney, the hotels and the campground. Signs make them easy to spot.

Phone cards are on sale at the post office in Festival Disney, in hotel shops, at the campground, at the golf course and in the following shops in the Park: Emporium, in Main Street, U.S.A.; Thunder Mesa Mercantile Building, in Frontierland; La Girafe Curieuse, in Adventureland; Sir Mickey's, in Fantasyland; Constellations, in Discoveryland. Minitel telephone keyboard service is available in each Euro Disney Resort hotel and Festival Disney. Mobile telecommunications systems can be rented from the hotels.

Newspapers, television and radio. International press can be found at newspaper stands at the RER station and in shops at the hotels.

The hotels and campground are connected to a cable-television network that lets you choose among a variety of international news, entertainment and sports channels. In-room televisions will also broadcast information about the Euro Disney Resort.

FM radio stations featuring mainly musical programmes are also available in the hotel rooms. An FM station, presented by Esso, broadcasts information about the Park and Resort area in three different languages.

SOME TIPS

Information. Inquire at the information booths in the Park:
— at Main Street Station and City Hall, in Main Street, U.S.A. (see p. 59).
— at Frontierland Depot, in Frontierland;
— opposite Trader Sam's Jungle Boutique, in Adventureland;
— in front of Alice's Curious Labyrinth, in Fantasyland.

Packing. Guests holidaying at the Euro Disney Resort are advised to bring comfortable clothing, in particular a pair of walking shoes, as well as evening clothes if they plan on dining in one of the Resort's elegant restaurants or going dancing. The list of articles not to forget also includes bathing suits and sportswear (tennis clothes and sweat pants, etc.).

When visiting the Park, it's better not to bring along too many cumbersome objects. Umbrellas, for instance, have an annoying habit of getting lost, so we suggest using the Mickey Mouse rain capes that can be bought at Plaza East and Plaza West Boutiques near the Main Entrance. Outside the Main Entrance, there's a left-luggage office for large and bulky items (Guest Storage). Inside, underneath Main Street Station, in Main Street, U.S.A., there are coin-operated storage lockers for storing coats, sweaters and purchases.

Photo-Video. In the Park, Kodak cameras and video cameras can be rented at Town Square Photography in Main Street, U.S.A.
You may also buy cameras and photographic equipment there and drop off your film for developing in two hours by Kodak. Pueblo Trading Post (Frontierland), Adventureland Bazar (Adventureland), Sir

Mickey's (Fantasyland) and Constellations (Discoveryland) all sell film and batteries. You can also get your film developed at these locations. The Kodak company has several locations throughout Euro Disneyland Park for choice photo opportunities. Look for the "Point Photo".
At the hotels and campground, film is developed in twenty-four hours.

Lost and Found. To report or claim a lost object in the Park, go to City Hall. If you've lost someone from your group, you may also leave a message there.

FIRST AID

Disney Parks are legendary for their high level of safety, and the Euro Disney Resort carries on the tradition. Cast Members receive special training that enables them to handle any situation that may arise. In case of emergency, a First Aid station staffed by registered nurses is located next to Plaza Gardens Restaurant on Central Plaza in the Park.

TRANSPORTATION

By car. The Guest Parking is huge, but you won't have any trouble finding your car, since the lot is handily divided into areas named after Disney characters. And if for some reason you should forget that your vehicle is parked in the Minnie area, a Cast Member will help you find it in no time at all. To get to the Park, take the moving sidewalks that run through the car park. The car park stays open until late at night, but cars cannot stay there overnight. Allow 30 F for a car, 20 F for a motorcycle, and 50 F for a caravan or camping car.

An Esso station is located near Hotel Santa Fe. In addition to the customary services, you'll find a car wash. The Europcar rental agency can be found at the same location. You can easily rent a car from your hotel and get a ride in a Europcar minibus to the agency. You can also book a rental car through the Euro Disney Central Reservations Office (see box p. 38).

If your car breaks down, report to the Security Cast Member.

Inside the Euro Disney Resort. A free shuttle-bus service taking guests throughout the grounds leaves about every ten minutes. The following three buses leave from the Gare Routière (bus station located between Festival Disney and the Disneyland Hotel, from which access to the Park and Festival Disney is very convenient):

— the first one stops off at Hotel New York, the Sequoia Lodge and the Newport Bay Club;

— the second one goes to Hotel Santa Fe and Hotel Cheyenne;

— the third one stops at the golf course and at the campground.

The Euro Disney Tram, with its striking blue-and-white roof and banners, provides complimentary transportation around the lake and stops at Festival Disney, the Newport Bay Club, the Sequoia Lodge and Hotel New York.

For guests in the Park, the Euro Disneyland Railroad is sure to be a treat for nostalgia lovers who dream about riding on a turn-of-the-century steam-engine train! The train makes a complete tour of the Park, offering passengers a glimpse of each land. There are three stations along the way, and you can go all the way around or get off whenever you please, either at Main Street Station, Frontierland Depot or Fantasyland Station. Between Main Street Station and Frontierland Depot, the train enters a magic tunnel-landscape, the Grand Canyon Diorama (see p. 74).

In Main Street, you can also take an authentic Horse-Drawn Streetcar or a turn-of-the-century vehicle at Main Street Vehicles to get from Town Square to Central Plaza (see pps. 59-60).

SHOPPING

In the Park and Festival Disney.
Unique and eclectic are the words to describe these shops, where you'll find everything from tee-shirts and delicate china to cowboy outfits and electronic video games. Mirroring the style of the land they're in, these shops are worth a visit if only just to see the decor. You won't want to miss seeing the antique cars for sale at Main Street Motors (see p. 63); asking Tigger at The Storybook Store to autograph your book (see p. 59); visiting the abandoned mine at the Eureka Mining Supplies and Assay Office (see p. 72) and the little beds overflowing with stuffed animals at

La Chaumière des Sept Nains (see p. 93); exploring the spaceship at Star Traders (see p. 108) and admiring Mickey Mouse in his *Ornithopter* at Constellations (see p. 104).

In the hotels. In the hotels, you'll find not only souvenirs but all kinds of useful items you may need in the course of your visit, including sunglasses, sun-care products, sandals, rain capes, film.

RESTAURANTS

In the Park, variety is also the name of the game when it comes to food. Menus offer fare from every country, designed to suit every kind of diet, all tastes, ages and budgets. Receptions and business or birthday banquets may also be arranged.

Restaurants, from the most simple to the most elegant, have been decorated with the utmost care in the style of the land in which they're located.

• The "castles". Restaurants in the Park are classified in three categories, from one to three "castles", depending on the services they offer.

— A "three-castle" establishment, the top level, offers you a special welcome and service with a personal touch, excellent cuisine and usually a show as well. Birthday cakes and special menus (low calorie, salt-free, etc...) may be ordered directly at the restaurant; group and kosher meals should be ordered in advance (inquire at City Hall or in the restaurants). Children have the choice between smaller portions of the standard menu or special meals all for themselves.

— "Two-castle" establishments offer counter service for those in a hurry. Children are offered "fun meals" with a main dish, milk product, dessert and... a surprise gift.

— "One-castle" establishments serve sandwiches, sausages, bagels, pretzels, etc. and refreshments.

• Chariots Gourmands. You'll run into numerous food and beverage carts in the Park called Chariots Gourmands, offering a variety of original snacks and refreshments (see the descriptions at the end of the sections on each land), as well as popcorn and ice-cream carts (hosted by Nestlé Ice Cream).

The hotels, Festival Disney and the campground offer you a choice among a wide variety of thematic restaurants featuring different styles of cuisine ranging from American home-style cooking to seafood dishes and southwestern specialties to name a few. A health-food dish of the day and dessert are available at all restaurants. Consult the restaurant index (p. 151 of the guidebook) for more help in making your choice.

A word to the wise: you'll have an easier time getting a table outside of the main French meal times (between 12 and 2 pm, and between 8 and 10 pm). If you plan on dining at a restaurant with table service, we recommend making reservations. Inquire at the restaurant of your choice.

SHOWS

In the Park. Each land has a number of outdoor shows that add to the festive air in the streets. In Main Street, U.S.A., you'll come across a town parade with a brass band, a pianist, and much more (see p. 67). In

Frontierland, the Riverboat Gamblers Dixieland Band will bid you farewell (see p. 73). In Adventureland, the Tam-Tams Africains will charm you, and you may run into Dr. Livingstone... But beware of pirates who appear out of the blue without warning (see p. 87)! In front of the charming buildings in Fantasyland, a lute player, jugglers, and best of all, Merlin the Magician (see p. 94) will be waiting for you. In Discoveryland, you'll see robots and futuristic musicians, and don't miss the Disney characters piloting bizarre flying machines (see p. 104).

Parades march by to the sound of splendid music, bringing the high points from Walt Disney animated films to life. The daytime parade goes through Fantasyland and down Main Street, U.S.A., twice a day during peak season and once during off season. At night, the Main Street Electrical Parade follows the same route (see p. 69).

Fantasia in the Sky is a spectacular fireworks show accompanied by the music from the famous animated film, *Fantasia*. For information about show times, pick up an entertainment brochure at the Main Entrance or at the information and exchange booths in the Park.

Some lands feature live entertainment illustrating their main theme, such as The Lucky Nugget Revue in Frontierland (see p. 75); *C'est Magique* and Le Théâtre du Château in Fantasyland (see p. 92); and Videopolis in Discoveryland (see p. 106).

NIGHTLIFE

Life at the Euro Disney Resort doesn't stop at sundown. There are numerous possibilities for night birds to enjoy themselves throughout the Resort, whether it be in the Park, at one of the hotels or in Festival Disney.

On the nights when the Theme Park is open late, guests can watch the Main Street Electrical Parade or go dancing in Discoveryland at the Videopolis discotheque (see p. 106).

In Festival Disney, dance lovers can also spend a whirlwind evening at Hurricanes discotheque (see p. 115).

In the hotel area, there is the dance floor at the Rainbow Lounge in Hotel New York for those who prefer something a little more intimate (see p. 126). And if you just feel like having a drink with friends, you can always go to one of the hotel bars which are open until late in the evening. There you can try one of the delicious cocktails, such as a traditional "sangria" or a "sombrero".

At the campground, country-music fans will enjoy listening to their favourite songs around the campfire.

Enjoying a taste of the nightlife at the Euro Disney Resort is the perfect way for guests to end their day, whether they've spent it enjoying themselves in the Euro Disneyland Park or attending meetings at the conference centre. And how about Parisians looking for a bit of relaxation and entertainment after a hard day's work in the city?

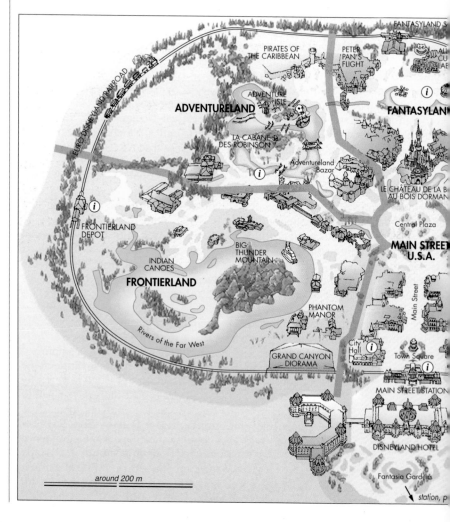

FANTASYLAND S

PIRATES OF
THE CARIBBEAN

PETER
PAN'S
FLIGHT

ALI
CU
LAE

EURO DISNEYLAND RAILROAD

ADVENTURE
ISLE

ADVENTURELAND

(i)

FANTASYLAN

LA CABANE
DES ROBINSON

Adventureland
Bazar

(i)

LE CHÂTEAU DE LA B
AU BOIS DORMAN

(i)

FRONTIERLAND
DEPOT

Central Plaza

INDIAN
CANOES

BIG
THUNDER
MOUNTAIN

MAIN STREE
U.S.A.

FRONTIERLAND

Main Street

PHANTOM
MANOR

Rivers of the Far West

City
Hall

(i)

Town Square

(i)

GRAND CANYON
DIORAMA

MAIN STREET STATION

around 200 m

DISNEYLAND HOTEL

Fantasia Gardens

station, p

A WORLD OF
PURE IMAGINATION

IT'S
A SMALL WORLD

STAR
TOURS

VIDEOPOLIS

CINÉMAGIQUE

ARIUM

DISCOVERYLAND

AUTOPIA

EURO DISNEYLAND RAILROAD

val Disney, hotels

Admission tickets here are called passports, and with good reason, because you'll be crossing a border to get inside, the one that separates the real world from the realm of the imaginary. It's a kingdom filled with fairies, dragons, pirates and flying elephants... where each step leads you into new adventures, unique encounters, and fabulous discoveries. You'll lose all notion of time. It's only natural... You've entered the world of dreams.

As soon as you enter Main Street, U.S.A., you'll be transported into another age, where the sound of horses' hooves and the clanking of a tramway in its tracks will remind you of an era when the fast lane hadn't been invented yet. The hustle and bustle of daily life, with its worries and cares, will fade as you start out on a carefree stroll through town.

And then you find yourself at Central Plaza, and the entrances to four

Minnie and a friend.

completely different and magical lands, where you'll feel like you've gone through the looking glass into the world of Walt Disney motion pictures. On the other side of reality everything will <u>seem</u> real to you, like in a dream that you wish would go on forever. There you'll meet legendary characters and will share adventures with them in Never Never Land.

In the streets of Fantasyland, your favourite Disney characters — Alice, Peter Pan, Merlin the Magician, Pinocchio and others — will smile and wave at you, to your own and your children's delight. At last you'll be

able to meet Cinderella... or Sleeping Beauty, whose castle towers majestically over the entrance to the land.

If you're the kind of person who loves going on expeditions, and revels in the strange and exotic, then plunge right into the Adventureland Bazar, and discover the islands, waterfalls, grottoes, caves, castaways and pirates of Adventureland beyond.

What of those who pine after an era when men and women had to face real dangers to stake out their claim?... In short, if you love westerns, then Frontierland is for you. Swagger through the swinging doors of The Lucky Nugget Saloon, the train will blow its whistle three times before you make up your mind to go wake up the spirits in the haunted mansion or explore the old gold mine.

If you're fascinated by the future and new technologies, don't feel left out — Discoveryland is the place for you! There you'll board the *Starspeeder 3000* on a voyage through the unknown corners of vast, intergalactic space. In this land, you'll discover the future as some of the great visionaries might have imagined it.

In the following pages we'll take you through each land, introducing you to the inhabitants, restaurants, shops, shows and attractions.

But you'll be amazed at all the other things there are to discover, especially the details of the architecture, decoration and costumes.

Each land creates an atmosphere appropriate to its theme with precision and imagination. Some items, such as the chariots on the Carrousel de Lancelot in Fantasyland and the mining tools in the Big Thunder Mountain gold mine in Frontierland, are real antiques.

Others are careful replicas that blend perfectly with their settings, such as the *moucharabies,* or Arab sculpted-wood windows, in Adventureland Bazar. At the Pirates of the Caribbean, the crumbling ramparts seem to have withstood the test of time and repeated enemy attacks. And what about the giant airship in Discoveryland, the Frontierland steamboats and the tramways of Main Street, U.S.A...

Are they the real thing? In the world of Disney they're as real as they can be, as real as Mickey Mouse's smile, as real as the fabulous landscapes full of canyons, deserts, lakes and rivers, and as real as the cactus and sequoia trees that have popped up out of nowhere in the heart of Ile-de-France.

These different elements combine to make Euro Disneyland Park another example of what Walt Disney dreamed of over 35 years ago: "A place where adults and children can experience together some of the wonders of life, of adventure, and feel better because of it".

The Main Street Electrical Parade.

55

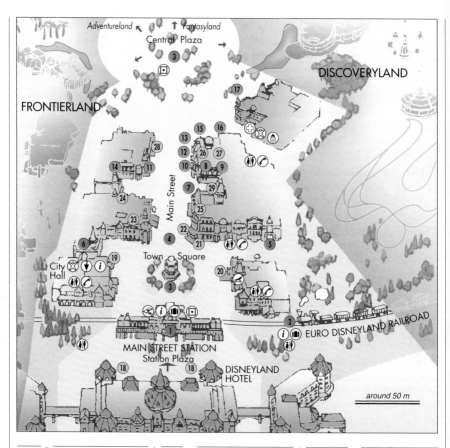

ATTRACTIONS

1. Main Street Station
2. Euro Disneyland Railroad
3. Horse-Drawn Streetcar
4. Main Street Vehicles
5. Discovery Arcade
6. Liberty Arcade
7. Main Street Motors

RESTAURANTS

8. The Ice Cream Company
9. The Coffee Grinder
10. Market House Deli
11. Walt's - an American Restaurant
12. Cable Car Bake Shop
13. Cookie Kitchen
14. Casey's Corner
15. The Gibson Girl Ice Cream Parlour
16. Victoria's Home-Style Cooking
17. Plaza Gardens Restaurant

SHOPS

18. Plaza West and Plaza East Boutiques
19. The Storybook Store
20. Ribbons & Bows Hat Shop
21. Town Square Photography/Silhouette Artist
22. Boardwalk Candy Palace
23. Emporium
24. Harmony Barber Shop
25. Disney Clothiers, Ltd.
26. Harrington's Fine China & Porcelains
27. Disneyana Collectibles
28. Disney & Co./Glass Fantasies
29. Newsstand

Main Street, U.S.A.

On Main Street you'll leave behind the hustle and bustle of the modern world and immerse yourself in the sounds and smells of the past.

All the antique charm of Victorian etchings has been restored in the splendid turn-of-the-century facades of Main Street, U.S.A. Arcades, shops and restaurants, gaslit street lamps and picturesque letter boxes bring back the romance of a forgotten era. Horse-drawn streetcars, omnibuses and other vehicles of the period pass up and down. With a view of the Château de la Belle au Bois Dormant, Main Street leads you directly into the heart of the enchanted realm of Walt Disney.

♥ Main Street Station ❶

When, as a young lad, Walt Disney sold newspapers on trains, he passed through stations just like this one. But now it's your journey which is about to begin...

There are storage lockers, located on the ground-floor level of the station, where you can deposit small items you don't want to carry with you. Then you can either enter Town Square and Main Street, U.S.A. or take the stairway up to the Euro Disneyland train for a grand tour of the Park.

♥ Euro Disneyland Railroad ❷

All three trains of the Euro Disneyland Railroad have five carriages and are pulled by steam engines.

Passengers on the Euro Disneyland Railroad.

The red, white and blue *George Washington* is similar to the Presidential trains used by the U.S. Government in the 19th century. The *W.F. Cody* is straight out of a Western. The third train, the *C.K. Holliday*, was inspired by trains that took holiday-makers to the East Coast

at the end of the 19th century. The carriages of each of the trains are named after early American cities — Yorktown, Chesapeake, Boston...

All aboard!... The stationmaster shouts, the engineer gives a blast on his whistle, and the train (carrying up to 270 passengers) is off on a tour of the Park. There are two stations en route, one in Frontierland, the other in Fantasyland. You'll pass through the untamed landscapes of the Grand Canyon Diorama (see p. 74), and then continue around the Park, with sneak previews of the exotic sights of Adventureland, the whimsical world of Fantasyland, and the futuristic architecture of Discoveryland...

Town Square. This charming little square has a well-kept lawn, flower beds, trees and benches, and in its centre, a gazebo. Interesting shops, the tramway depot and City Hall border the square, with Main Street Station on its southern side. At Christmastime, the tree in the centre of the square is ablaze with fairy lights and decorations.

Guided Tours (see p. 34) start from The Arboretum on the western side of the square.

🎁 Plaza West and Plaza East Boutiques ⑱

(See p. 34.)

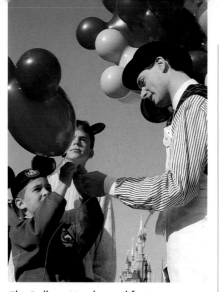

The Balloon Vendor and fans.

City Hall. This stately building, furnished with antiques and a marble reception counter, is the main information centre of the Euro Disneyland Park. The programmes of the shows presented in the different lands and the departure times for the Guided Tours are available here, and you'll be able to obtain all the information you need to make your visit more enjoyable. On the wall, there's a huge map of the Park to help you find your way around, and you can obtain full information on the hotels, the camp site and Festival Disney. Inquire here about lost children; they can be retrieved from the Baby Care Center, located next to Plaza Gardens Restaurant. Lost property can be retrieved at the Lost & Found counter here at City Hall.

The Storybook Store ⑲ This bookshop resembles a library of the early 1900s. There's a warm and friendly atmosphere and more than a touch of fantasy. The shelves are brimming with books available in different languages, storytelling cassettes and an assortment of stationery items. An amiable Tigger is there to stamp your children's books with the date of their visit and the Euro Disneyland logo.

Ribbons & Bows Hat Shop ⑳ This attractive little shop has a superb collection of hats and accessories inspired by Victorian fashion. Display cabinets, old-fashioned hat boxes, and round baskets are filled with hats of all shapes and sizes as well as bows, ribbons, hair slides and combs. At the back of the shop there's a workshop with old-fashioned sewing machines. You may have your name embroidered on the hat of your choice.

Main Street Vehicles ❹ (presented by Europcar). Main Street just wouldn't be Main Street without the wailing of sirens, the spluttering of car engines, and the blaring of klaxon horns.

All kinds of vehicles pass up and down the street, and you can choose the type of transport that suits your taste. Climb aboard the police Paddy

One of the many Main Street, U.S.A. vehicles.

Wagon or, if you prefer the company of firemen, hop onto the Fire Truck. If you want to get a good view as you travel, then you'll probably prefer riding on the top deck of the Omnibus. Or if you really want to live it up, then snap up the chauffeur's invitation to ride down Main Street in a luxurious Limousine. And don't forget to record these moments for posterity with a photograph, either at the start of your trip or behind the wheel of one of the two turn-of-the-century antique vehicles parked in the street.

The Horse-Drawn Streetcar.

Horse-Drawn Streetcar ③

Pulled by strong Percheron horses, these authentic streetcars, with colourful old-style advertising on either side, bring to life the old illustrations of America's first public-transport system. Boarding at Town Square, you'll ride slowly up Main Street as far as Central Plaza to the clip-clop of horses' hooves and the screeching of metal wheels. Those were the days...

The Euro Disneyland Band marching down Main Street.

Discovery Arcade ⑤

This arcade runs along the east side of Main Street from Town Square Photography to The Gibson Girl Ice Cream Parlour and gives you access to the rear entry of the shops and restaurants. Discovery Arcade is dedicated to the imaginative spirit of people everywhere. In the display cabinets, you'll see scaled-down models, sketches and mock-ups of flying machines, cars and trains, plus the plans of past and present American cities. Superb gas lamps, the supporting columns and their coloured tiles all contribute to the character and charm of this passageway.

Liberty Arcade ⑥

On the west side of Main Street stretching as far as the entrance to Frontierland, this arcade pays tribute to the Statue of Liberty, that great lady who welcomes immigrants to New York Harbor, and is a symbol famous the world over. Plans, drawings and photographs retrace her history from the first sketches by its designer Bartholdi to the Franco-American restoration work.

In the heart of the arcade is **Liberty Court** (which can also be reached via Flower Street) where you'll find the

60

Statue of Liberty Tableau, a huge diorama which winds back the clock to the night of October 28th, 1886, when the statue was unveiled. To the sound of *Hail to the Chief* and *La Marseillaise*, you'll relive this historic event as if you were one of the actual guests who, packed together on the bridge of a ship, gazed through the evening mist at Liberty "enlightening the world".

A mosaic beneath your feet shows exactly where the statue is located in New York Harbor.

🎁 Town Square Photography ㉑

(hosted by Kodak). This shop is a veritable museum of photographic paraphernalia displaying many fore-runners of today's equipment — tripods, old-fashioned camera cases and many other items, lovingly collected and arranged. Here, you can buy film, photographic equipment and lenses at the counter or hire regular and video cameras. If you're in a hurry to admire yourself alongside Mickey Mouse or Snow White, you won't have to wait long — your film will be developed and printed in two hours (see also p. 48).

You may want to stop just inside the shop to have your portrait snipped from a piece of paper by the **Silhouette Artist.**

Here, as in the Harmony Barber Shop, Market House Deli and Casey's Corner, you'll find a telephone — if you pick it up, you can listen in on the private conversations of a few inhabitants of Main Street, U.S.A. This re-creates the time when, in the United States, people shared party lines and it was often necessary to wait until someone else finished his or her conversation before making a call.

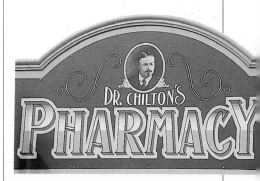

A sign in Main Street, U.S.A.

🎁 Boardwalk Candy Palace ㉒

(hosted by Nestlé). It's as if you were strolling along the seaside promenade in Atlantic City a hundred years ago. Your nostrils suddenly begin to quiver at the deliciously sweet smells wafting through the air. Unable to resist, you trace the scent and step inside the Boardwalk Candy Palace. The walls of this sweet shop are covered with murals of jetties stretching out into the ocean. Around the ceiling, there's a frieze depicting

The omnibus with its top deck.

The shop is lit by a huge chandelier and natural light which comes from the dome. Suspended from the ceiling is a working reproduction of an old pneumatic system of little baskets into which cashiers put money to be sent to a central cash desk and then returned with correct change and a receipt. There are old-style advertising posters of the Emporiums at both Disneyland Park and Walt Disney World Resort. In the Emporium's several departments you can buy decorative gifts, jewellery, men's and women's clothes and accessories, toys, fluffy animals and video cassettes.

all sorts of sweets. Blown-glass columns contain candy. In this veritable paradise for those with a sweet tooth, there are sweets everywhere...

"Lucy the glass elephant" is topped up with them, and so is a huge Ferris wheel and dozens of glass jars. Children will have fun flattening their noses to the windows of the kitchen to gaze at the candymakers preparing fudge, peanut brittle and chocolate-covered strawberries. Chocolates in refrigerated display cabinets are sold by weight or by the piece. You can also buy saltwater taffy and old-fashioned sweet tins in the shape of Disney characters.

Emporium ㉓ You'll find Emporium, the Park's largest shop, on the corner of Main Street and Town Square.

It houses several shops including The Toy Chest and Bixby Brothers. Classic Disney characters decorate the windows. On the stained-glass domed ceiling, you'll see a series of portraits paying tribute to eight famous inventors.

Harmony Barber Shop ㉔ A men's barber shop just like they used to be, with mirrors, posters, newspapers and barber's "tools" of the period. Leather strap, razor and brush in hand, the barber is ready to settle you into the revolving chair for a trim or a "perfect" shave. There are shaving brushes, razors and other accessories for sale.

For youngsters who experience their first haircut, there's a great souvenir certificate with a picture of Goofy.

The Main Street Quartet sings traditional barbershop quartet songs.

Disney Clothiers, Ltd. ㉕ This sumptuous drapery was converted from an old private house; there's a flat at the back of the shop with a sewing room (equipped with mannequin) and a parlour with a player piano. There's a range of fashion items in the shop's authentic display cabinets including Disney clothes and accessories for the entire family. On the mezzanine floor, you'll find a range of clothing to suit the most refined tastes.

Main Street Motors ❼ (presented by Esso). A petrol pump dating back to 1916 with a glass reservoir standing on the edge of the footpath, huge advertising hoardings outside — you're at your local car dealer. Inside the showroom, with its black and white tiled floor, original posters and a series of photographs depict the legend of the American automobile and the first mass-production models. Three vintage cars and a motorbike are displayed on a wooden dais. You can simply admire them or, should one take your fancy, you can buy it on the spot! An inexhaustible salesman vaunts the qualities of these classics. If you find these models a little beyond your pocket, there's always the metal reproductions of antique models, enamelled numberplates, posters and postcards.

Newsstand ㉙ On Main Street, as in most turn-of-the-century American towns, you'll find a newsstand displaying newspapers and magazines from bygone days.

The Ice Cream Company ❽ (hosted by Nestlé Ice Cream). At the lower end of Market Street, the

tiled counters of The Ice Cream Company open onto the street and Discovery Arcade. From cabinets which were originally topped up with salt crystals to keep them cold, you can choose a delicious American-style ice cream in your favourite flavour, served in a cone or in small cups with biscuits in the shape of Disney characters.

Tables and chairs are provided outside on Market Street, with all sorts of delicacies displayed in barrows and baskets.

The Coffee Grinder ❾ (hosted by Nescafé). As you walk down Main Street, the aroma of fresh coffee will undoubtedly lure you into this charming coffee house. In among the early coffee grinders and the sacks of coffee beans, a vintage espresso machine sits proudly on the counter. In the red-toned ceramic setting, waiters offer you a choice of freshly ground coffees with a variety of toppings and pastries.

If you prefer, you can sit outside on the terrace which looks onto Main Street.

Market House Deli ⑩

You'll find this cosy old-fashioned general store on the corner of Market Street and Main Street. There are sausages hanging from the ceiling, racks full of jams and preserves, an old cast-iron stove which warms the shop in winter, barrels of pickles and a player piano. At the counter, you may buy made-to-order American-style hot or cold sandwiches (pastrami, ham, turkey, cheese, on your choice of bread). Call the "olive and pickle man" to your table for an extra taste treat! You can either sit inside or on the terrace and order a slice of an amazing, 2-m-long "submarine" sandwich.

Walt's - an American Restaurant ⑪

Partly an art gallery paying tribute to Walt Disney, this is one of the most elegant restaurants in Euro Disneyland Park. It may interest you to know that Walt's Restaurant has the same address as the workshops of Walt Disney Imagineering in Glendale, California (1401 Flower Street), and that the logo with the initials W.D. appearing on the gas lamps and windows was designed for the balcony of Walt's Disneyland apartment.

On the ground floor there's an elegant bistro. On the walls, photographs honouring Walt Disney retrace his childhood his youth, his early days as a cartoonist and his career as a film maker, including reproductions from his first animated motion pictures. The menu, which doubles as a photo album of his life, is presented to each visitor.

You'll also find a zoetrope; by turning the handle of this device, you'll see Mickey Mouse as he appeared in the 1930s.

As you make your way up the stairs, take time to peruse the wonderful photographs on the landings.

The first-floor restaurant is divided into several small dining rooms representing the lands of Euro Disneyland Park.

Fantasyland is depicted in Gothic style, and the Château de la Belle au Bois Dormant is portrayed on the hangings.

Frontierland is represented by the library of an old western mansion, Adventureland by a kind of eclectic Moroccan parlour, and Discoveryland by a fantasy setting around a model of Captain Nemo's *Nautilus* in copper. You can also dine on the outdoor terrace.

Dapper waiters offer you a choice from the very best in American cuisine — salad dressed with specially made apple-cider dressing, shrimp scampi, grilled salmon, crabcakes, Alaskan crab legs, veal medallions with crab and asparagus, lamb with goat's cheese...

Harrington's Fine China & Porcelains 26

The refined tastefulness of Harrington's makes it stand out among the other shops on Main Street. The luxurious rounded interior is enhanced by marble statues, magnificent carpets, neo-classical columns and a crystal chandelier hangs from the stained-glass domed roof. A wide variety of valuable objects are displayed in mahogany cabinets — chinaware, crystal glasses, precious stones, antique statuettes and a range of English tea services. Sitting by the entrance, a craftsman finishes by hand items for the visitors.

Disneyana Collectibles 27

This shop, designed to please the keenest of Disney fans, is an extension of Harrington's. A statue of Mickey Mouse, standing in the centre dressed as a magician, welcomes the visitors. Collectors will find a selection of unique memorabilia, jewellery boxes, rare books, ceramic figures, limited-edition lithographs and the celluloids used in some of the most famous Walt Disney motion pictures.

Cable Car Bake Shop 12

Attracted by the enticing aromas wafting through the air, you decide to pop into the bakery... and you find yourself in old San Francisco! Photographs of trams and steeply sloped streets dot the walls, plunging you right into the heart of this legendary city. You'll even see a toy cable car circulating on a track above your head. Put your eye to the Cail-o-scope viewer and you'll see pictures of the dreadful earthquake that devastated the city in 1906. A ventilator and a pot-bellied stove set the tone of this traditional bakery where, each day, bakers prepare chocolate cookies, brownies, cheesecake and other typically American cakes. These goodies are served (with espresso coffee if you wish) at the counter and you may enjoy them at one of the many tables.

Cookie Kitchen 13

The delicious-looking cookies being prepared in full view of the passers-by will make you want to stop at this counter located next to the Cable Car Bake Shop. Although cookies are the specialty, try their muffins, cinnamon rolls and juices.

Disney & Co. 28

Toys, cuddly animals and clothes bearing the likeness of Disney characters are displayed in a decor which re-creates a fairground at the turn of the century. Look at Mickey Mouse and Minnie Mouse waving from the hot air balloon.

Located inside Disney & Co., **Glass Fantasies** features an artisan creating knitted-glass giftware before your very eyes.

Plaza Gardens Restaurant.

Casey's Corner ⑭ (hosted by Coca-Cola). A wooden replica of a baseball player at the entrance invites passers-by into Casey's Corner, dedicated to America's "national pastime". The restaurant, decorated in honour of the game, has

The Jungle Book — part of the Daily Parade.

a sculpted wooden frieze made up of bats, balls, pennants and trophies. Try your luck against an entire field on veteran pinball machines. You can order hot dogs or chili dogs from the player-waiters at a counter lit by Tiffany lamps. Drinks and snacks are listed on a huge scoreboard behind the counter. Sit inside or on the outside patio and listen to the **Ragtime Piano Player and Banjo Player.** The musicians, also dressed in baseball gear, set the visitors' feet tapping with a medley of old American ragtime and sing-alongs.

The Gibson Girl Ice Cream Parlour ⑮ (hosted by Nestlé Ice Cream). This temple of ice cream is dedicated to the celebrated drawings by Charles D. Gibson of its glamorous and voluptuous namesake. Besides a jukebox, chairs with heart-shaped backs and marble tabletops, the parlour boasts an authentic soda fountain. You can choose from sundaes, milk shakes and banana splits or, if you're really hungry, try the "kitchen sink", big enough for four, with many different scoops of ice cream topped with sauces, whipped cream, candied fruit and nuts to taste.

The counter girls are in button-up boots and long frilled dresses, evoking Gibson's image of the thoroughly "modern" woman.

Victoria's Home-Style Cooking ⑯ Victoria, the proprietor of this 1890s-style boarding house, has put all her culinary know-how to the service of her guests. Sit in front of the dining room fireplace, by the organ or cast-iron stove in the curio-filled living room, or even among the plants and birdcages of the conser-

The Ragtime Piano Player.

vatory. If you look through the hatch behind the service counter, you'll see Victoria's enormous oven from which emerge her delicious "pot pies", made with either chicken, beef, seafood or vegetables. Guests can eat inside, or on the patio which Victoria's shares with The Gibson Girl Ice Cream Parlour.

Plaza Gardens Restaurant ⑰
(hosted by Nestlé). On arriving at Central Plaza, you'll notice a building with a veranda running the length of its facade. Its wide bay windows look through into a splendid restaurant designed in the typical grand and elegant architectural style of the 19th

At the entrance to Main Street, U.S.A., Mickey Mouse and Minnie Mouse, Donald Duck, Daisy, Goofy, Pluto and Chip an' Dale are likely to be there to provide a cheery welcome for the visitors.
And, as you walk on up the street, you'll meet many more surprising characters...

Main Street Quartet. This barbershop quartet sings up and down Main Street, stopping on street corners, and occasionally hopping onto a passing tram. Dressed in striped waistcoats, long aprons and boaters, they sing traditional barbershop-quartet songs.

Keystone Kops. Siren wailing, a police paddy wagon turns onto Main Street. On board, a saxophone quintet in police uniforms with gold badges on their caps plays a selection of arresting silent-movie tunes.

The Suffragettes. Dressed for a protest march in the days when they still didn't have voting rights, this all-women band plays a selection of rousing turn-of-the-century airs...

century. Two large murals bring to life scenes of winter and summer in a park during Victorian times. Decorated with antique furniture and china, Plaza Gardens is divided into two dining rooms, each with columns and glass roofs, and has two additional private rooms. Marble statues bearing candelabra invite you to move towards the large buffets covered with hot and cold dishes. Fresh fruit in season is presented on a revolving fountain in the middle of the room along with two marble counters laid out with desserts. A little further off, roast chicken, salmon, crabcakes, veal breast stuffed with fruit and American-style steaks are being prepared in the rotisserie and grill sections. You can also dine outside, either on the terrace or on the veranda. The **Plaza Gardens Trio** is made up of three proper Victorian ladies who entertain you with delightful chamber music.

Chariot Gourmand. The **Bagel Cart** serves — as its name implies — bagels, toasted in front of you and offered with a choice of six toppings, including one which is sweet, one for vegetarians and one low-fat.

Fantasia in the Sky, *an unforgettable fireworks display.*

THE PARADES

The Euro Disneyland Parades march between It's a Small World and Town Square, passing in front of the castle, around Central Plaza and down Main Street. Parade times and frequencies vary according to the season, so please inquire at the Main Entrance, City Hall and information booths throughout the Park.

Daytime Parade. This procession of scenes and characters from well-known Disney motion pictures is led by the Fantasyland Fanfares. First comes Sleeping Beauty, riding on a float built to look exactly like her castle. Beside her, the three fairies are huddled around Princess Aurora's cradle. Majestic music ushers in a long procession of valets carrying banners, jugglers, knights on horseback, courtiers and ladies-in-waiting. And, high above them, the 5-m-tall Maleficent. Then you'll see the Prince battling with the Dragon to get to the Princess and wake her with a kiss. Next comes Geppetto in his workshop with Pinocchio and Jiminy Cricket. Snow White, accompanied by the Seven Dwarfs, is just ahead of Cinderella in her crystal coach. Behind her, Dumbo does little pirouettes in the air and Peter Pan sways along on a pirate ship with booming cannons. Then you'll flip through the pages of the *Jungle Book* with elephants and Bagheera the panther. Eric and Ariel, the Little Mermaid, float along in an underwater scene, while Roger Rabbit and Eddie are close behind in Benny the Cab. Mickey Mouse is the special star of the Grand Finale, riding in his amazing rocket ship and joined by all the other characters in wacky flying machines.

Main Street Electrical Parade (presented by Philips). Thousands of twinkling lights pass through Fantasyland and Main Street, U.S.A. in this nighttime parade of seventy-three performers in luminous costumes.

In order of appearance, you'll see: the Blue Fairy from Pinocchio; a train driven by Goofy with Mickey Mouse sitting atop a giant bass drum ; Alice in a Wonderland inhabited by snails, centipedes, flying beetles, and giant mushrooms.

Then there's the circus with its crazy menagerie sporting a honey bear, and King Lion playing the calliope, followed by Elliot, the fire-breathing dragon, the children of It's a Small World and finally Cinderella's coach followed by a clock which chimes out the twelve strokes of midnight.

Little kids (and even the most blasé big kids) will be dazzled by this brilliant spectacle.

Fireworks. The *Fantasia in the Sky* fireworks display transports you into the enchantment of the famous Walt Disney motion picture *Fantasia*. For five exciting minutes, the sky above the castle bursts into a blaze of multicoloured light to the sound of the familiar soundtrack themes.

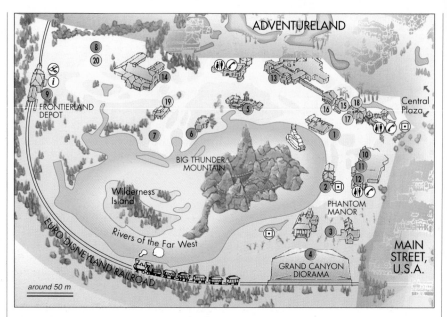

ADVENTURELAND

FRONTIERLAND DEPOT

Central Plaza

BIG THUNDER MOUNTAIN

Wilderness Island

Rivers of the Far West

EURO DISNEYLAND RAILROAD

PHANTOM MANOR

GRAND CANYON DIORAMA

MAIN STREET, U.S.A.

around 50 m

ATTRACTIONS

① Rustler Roundup Shootin' Gallery
② Thunder Mesa Riverboat Landing
③ Phantom Manor
④ Grand Canyon Diorama
⑤ Big Thunder Mountain
⑥ River Rogue Keelboats
⑦ Indian Canoes
⑧ Cottonwood Creek Ranch/Critter Corral
⑨ Frontierland Depot

RESTAURANTS

⑩ The Lucky Nugget Saloon
⑪ Last Chance Cafe
⑫ Silver Spur Steakhouse
⑬ Fuente del Oro Restaurante
⑭ Cowboy Cookout Barbecue

SHOPS

⑮ Thunder Mesa Mercantile Building
⑯ Tobias Norton & Sons – Frontier Traders
⑰ Bonanza Outfitters
⑱ Eureka Mining Supplies and Assay Office
⑲ Pueblo Trading Post
⑳ Woodcarver's Workshop

*F*rontierland

As you enter Frontierland, you journey back to the time when dreams of newfound wealth and unconquered wilderness beckoned settlers to venture west of the Rocky Mountains. You'll see sweeping landscapes of plains and canyons, and rivers dotted with colourful steamboats and Indian canoes. In the little town of Thunder Mesa, where the Wild West comes alive as it was in the late 1800s, you'll meet pioneers and see mementos of the gold rush. The glory — and decadence — of these legendary days is relived through a "French cancan", a visit to a haunted house, or a ride through an old gold mine!

If you're coming from Central Plaza, you can reach Frontierland by following the dirt path leading to Fort Comstock. You can also enter via covered walkways from Main Street, U.S.A., or Adventureland.

Fort Comstock. The first pioneers of Thunder Mesa needed the log enclosure of this old stockade for protection — but no need to panic, there's no danger. The Indians won't attack you, and the lookout post, once occupied by armed men, is now equipped only with telescopes through which you can scan the countryside; from here you'll get a fine view of the whole of Frontierland.

Thunder Mesa Mercantile Building ⓕ
Wooden boardwalks, rustic shop fronts, signboards and old-style ads... You're suddenly in the very special atmosphere of an old Far West town, with the clamour of stagecoaches and horses' hooves resounding from Thunder Mesa Road to Lucky Nugget Lane. The town's three best-known shops are all housed under one roof, evidence of Thunder Mesa's prosperity. The gold mine's success gave the local traders a huge boost, and the shop windows are brimming with the most sought-after goods in the West.

Tobias Norton & Sons - Frontier Traders ⓰
The timber decor of this reputable establishment takes you back to the glorious days of the trappers, when furs were exchanged for gold at the height of the boom. There are hunting trophies and relics of the Wild West above the stone fireplace, where Kit Carson and Buffalo Bill probably warmed themselves on their return from the Great Plains. Here too, nomadic tribes of Cheyenne Indians traded hand-crafted moccasins and leather pouches for food staples like flour and sugar.

Bonanza Outfitters ⓱
This large store, catering to Western males and females, is sophisticated and roomy. You can see lifelike replicas of cowboys from a cattle drive — some leaning on saddles, others on piles of blankets — against a background of painted landscapes above dark timber shelves. While you wander around the store, an imperturbable Mountain Man seems to be keeping his eye on you from the back of the shop. Take your pick: boots, scarves, gun belts, jeans, fringed shirts, hats, accessories in silver and turquoise — everything to equip you to conquer the wide-open spaces.

Eureka Mining Supplies and Assay Office ⓲
This toy shop is located on the site of a former gold mine where some of its ruins can still be seen, such as an enormous iron hoist and machines connected by iron fittings. You can buy cowboy and goldminer's outfits, sheriff's badges, toy-rifle replicas, hats and cuddly animals — all on show in the loaded ore cars. While the antique scales used for weighing the gold nuggets can still be seen, jars of old-fashioned candy have replaced the miners' tools in the showcases under the main counter — and don't miss the rattlesnake meat, the buffalo pâté and other Western foods.

Rustler Roundup Shootin' Gallery ❶
A timber warehouse on the bank of the river houses a specialty of Arizona — the rifle range. You can choose a vintage rifle and

The Big Thunder Mountain Mining Company.

test your marksmanship. There's no shortage of targets — bottles, tombstones, bank robbers — and the results can be pretty surprising! Aim at the dynamite shack, and the door is blown off; hit the chicken's perch, and an egg drops down into a basket. There are more than twenty targets scattered throughout the landscape... so, amid the noise, why not test your shooting skills?

(Don't forget — there is an additional charge for this attraction.)

Rivers of the Far West. A network of rivers is woven through the prairies and forests of Frontierland. All sorts of craft cruise the waterways: canoes, keelboats and the big steam-powered riverboats. Each bend in the river traces out the story of the gold rush and the conquest of the West.

Thunder Mesa Riverboat Landing ❷ Here, at this covered, open-air landing, you can choose from one of two riverboats, the *Mark Twain* or the *Molly Brown*, to take you on a tour of the Rivers of the Far West. From your boat, you'll see the steep-sided cliffs and arid landscapes of Big Thunder Mountain; Wilderness Island with its forests and waterfalls; and the mud flats, with a geyser spouting over twenty metres into the air. A blast on the ship's whistle, and the romantic voyage through the Western waterways has begun.

At the dock, dressed in bright jackets, floral waistcoats, coloured boots and boaters, the **Riverboat Gamblers Dixieland Band** bids farewell to the boats with well-loved New Orleans jazz tunes.

Which boat will you choose? The graceful *Mark Twain* with her huge paddle wheel on the stern churning up the water? Or maybe you'll go for the *Molly Brown*... propelled by two paddle wheels, one on either side, with a walking-beam engine providing her power.

The stylish flair for detail is apparent in the cabins of both boats, from the refined drapery and lacework at the windows to the elegant upholstery of the armchairs. Leaning over the rails of one of these two grand old riverboats, you'll savour the charm of the America of yesteryear.

Phantom Manor ❸ This lofty, deserted old mansion surrounded by brambles stands as a sinister shadow of its former splendid glory. A remnant of the times when fortunes were made — and lost — overnight, it reflects the luxurious lifestyle of its former owner who had it built in high Victorian style. And what's left of it now? Not the slightest sign of life, except perhaps for a wisp of greenish smoke coming from a chimney, and the flickering of a candle flame in one of the windows. You're caught between wanting to know more and the dread this gloomy place emanates. But temptation will win out and you enter as if in a dream. Now dream turns to nightmare as doors swing shut behind you, the walls close in on you and begin to change their shape. You board one of the small vehicles which makes its way from room to room through dark corridors and ominous catacombs. Mocking laughter echoes around you, ghouls dance, transparent figures glide past, stifled groans mingle with crashing organ chords... "Come back soon" cries a ghost as, quivering with fear, you finally emerge from this tormented place.

And now, if the spirit is still willing, you can visit the nearby cemetery, **Boot Hill**, to contemplate the family graves and decipher the epitaphs inscribed on the gravestones, the coffins and the walls of the crypt.

Inside Phantom Manor.

Grand Canyon Diorama ❹ Halfway between Main Street Station and the Frontierland Depot, the Euro Disneyland Railroad (see p. 58) enters a tunnel.

You are now in the Grand Canyon Diorama, a highly realistic tableau which takes you through a day along the rim of the celebrated natural wonder. Dazzling effects are used to reproduce flora and fauna and a vast array of natural sounds and phenomena. From your carriage, you will see a panorama of events stretching from dawn till dusk — a spectacular storm, a rainbow, and a glorious sunset. You'll see the remnants of an ancient Indian cliff dwelling, antelopes scrambling over rocks, and take a coyote by surprise. You'll come across a rattlesnake, a herd of deer, an owl descending towards its prey. At the end of this spectacular experience, you will emerge to the "reality" of Big Thunder Mountain, towering over the Rivers of the Far West.

The Lucky Nugget Saloon ❿ Walk through swinging doors into plenty of noise and clamour — you've just stepped into The Lucky Nugget... It's a genuine Far West saloon down to the last detail: horseshoe-shaped and laid out like a theatre, with stage, balcony and velvet-curtained boxes.

Diamond Lil, proprietress of The Lucky Nugget Saloon.

Connected to Main Street, U.S.A. by an arcade, The Lucky Nugget is one of the oldest buildings in Thunder Mesa. Bought by Diamond Lil with a down payment of an enormous gold nugget, today it houses a stage and a restaurant. Amid the red and gold decor, waitresses clad in "French cancan"-style costumes will offer you a choice of delicious sandwiches for lunch, or when it's time for dinner, the traditional spareribs or grilled chicken, oven-baked potatoes, and corn on the cob followed by hot apple crumble with ice cream.

The Lucky Nugget Revue. Presented for you by Diamond Lil in collaboration with Pierre Paradis (a Frenchman she met on one of her trips to Europe), the show blends together a whole host of talent with comedy, melodrama and *vaudeville* on the bill. Charlie McGee, Lil's old friend from her gold-mining days, comes down from the hills to join in the fun. Lil is up there on stage alongside six dancers and actors specially imported from the Old World. The girls, feathers in their hair and clad in fishnet stockings, petticoats and red shoes, open the show with a "French cancan" and end up among the guests for the rousing finale. The show lasts approximately 30 minutes, with lots of laughs and plenty of songs.

Please inquire at The Lucky Nugget Saloon for show times and reservations.

Last Chance Cafe ⑪ Located between The Lucky Nugget Saloon and the Silver Spur Steakhouse, this café is also a gallery of wanted posters of outlaws and desperados. But don't let this stop you from going up to the counter to order a Texan sandwich that you can enjoy eating on the terrace with a view of Big Thunder Mountain.

A windmill in Frontierland.

Silver Spur Steakhouse ⑫

Located right across from the Riverboat Landing, this is undeniably the most elegant building in Thunder Mesa. In the 1880s, it was the favourite place for wealthy cattle barons and eminent townspeople to meet, in surroundings which reflected their affluence. The tone is set by chandeliers, ornate chairs upholstered in cowhide, crystal bowls, pewter and copper lamps, elaborate mahogany panels and luxurious velvet curtains. An extra touch of refinement is provided by antiques and paintings, sculptures and bronzes by well-known Western artists. You will be greeted by your host in his red-collared frock coat, and your hostess in a long draped dress. At the table, you can select from a prime-rib, T-bone steak, choice cuts of lamb, pork, chicken, or fish; your choice is grilled in an open kitchen allowing you to watch the entire process.

Fuente del Oro Restaurante ⑬

Every day's a fiesta in this cheerful Mexican cantina. In the middle of the large patio an ancient Mayan fountain gurgles gently against a background of the guitar, trumpet, and violin serenade of the **Fuente del Oro Mariachis** in their wide black sombreros, short jackets and fringed pants. The bright colours of the facade are echoed in the ochre of the terracotta floor, the Mexican-style doors and bar, and the brocade costumes of the waiters. The festival atmosphere is increased by the ritual preparation of fajitas, chicken or beef, and thinly-sliced vegetables, cooked on a hot sizzler plate. Of course you can try any of the Mexican specialties such as tacos, chili con carne, the Mexican Club Sandwich made with guacamole, refried beans, tomatoes, and cheese, or enjoy a non-alcoholic Margarita or Mexican coffee. All dishes are served at the counter, but you might want to sit under the arbour bordering the patio in the courtyard or in the open-fronted dining room.

Big Thunder Mountain ⑤

Monument Valley in the heart of the Rivers of the Far West! Big Thunder re-creates the majestic scenery of the American Southwest with rocky peaks almost touching the sky, red hills, canyons and wind-swept plateaus. The mountains are brought to life with perfect replicas of the flora and fauna of this region. The blast of dynamite used by the gold-miners in their search for wealth still echoes off the walls of this rugged terrain.

Big Thunder Mountain.

There's nothing in all Frontierland quite so adventurous as the ride through this weird and wonderful landscape in the runaway mine train... On the platform of an old mine, an ex-miner will warn you of the hazards of the journey you are about to undertake. No sooner has the train pulled out, than down it plunges into a mine shaft, goes under the river, then

rattles up to the surface inside the mountain, and on through the caverns of the old mine, glistening with stalactites and phosphorescent pools. It picks up speed and comes out through a mining camp into a pine-wood forest. Before you've time to catch your breath, you go diving back down at breakneck speed into the gloom of the most dangerous section of the mine — where they're still blasting! "No Smoking" signs are pasted on the cases of dynamite.

Disaster strikes ! A huge blast, then one explosion after another goes echoing through the adjacent mine shafts. Sections of the roof come crumbling down, finally uncovering one of the richest veins of gold in the history of the Big Thunder Mine. But the gold turns to dust and disappears into the cracks in the rock as you resurface, breathless, at the end of this fantastic journey to disembark at Big Thunder Mining Company Headquarters.

River Rogue Keelboats ❻ The dock at Smuggler's Cove is carefully hidden and you'll board by

torch light for a river cruise. This is where smugglers stashed away their crates of whisky and stolen hides. But these old rogues have plenty of spare time and they're happy to welcome you on one of their two boats, the *Coyote* or the *Raccoon*, reminiscent of the craft which used to punt up and down the rivers of the West back in the early 19th century. Sitting at water level, you'll be taken along the Rivers of the Far West, weaving in and out of the washes of passing paddle steamers, skillfully guided by an enthusiastic river rogue.

Pueblo Trading Post.

Indian Canoes ❼ Not far from the Pueblo Trading Post, you proceed down a tree-lined sandstone path to a narrow slip in the river. Here you board an Indian Canoe for an adventurous passage through the Rivers of the Far West. In the canoes, there's enough room for twenty people plus two guides. Paddle in hand, you're off to discover the secrets of these Rivers in places where no other boat can make its way.

You'll be skirting Wilderness Island, passing by waterfalls and gliding under graceful Rainbow Arch. Then, just before arriving back at the boarding point, you'll slip through a narrow passage formed by the natural erosion from the wind and rain at the base of Big Thunder Mountain. Crossing the Rivers, you head back to disembark at the Indian Canoe landing.

All aboard the Euro Disneyland Railroad.

Pueblo Trading Post ⑲
This small shop, built from ochre-coloured New Mexico clay, has a brightly decorated entry shaded by a timber awning. Here you'll find the traditional handicrafts of the Navajo and Hopi Indians — an array of pottery, hand-woven Indian blankets and carpets, silver and turquoise jewellery, flutes, and dolls.

Cottonwood Creek Ranch ⑧
Far from the hubbub of the town, the Cottonwood Creek Ranch introduces you to farming country. Here, the days are long and work doesn't stop until sundown. It's a good idea to take a break at **Critter Corral** across from the scarecrow in the middle of the cornfields, close to the mill; budding cowboys can approach and pet the animals (goats, sheep, ducks, chickens and rabbits).

Woodcarver's Workshop ⑳
Close by the Ranch, in a small workshop packed with all sorts of tools, a craftsman is carving little wooden animals. Why not ask him to make one to take with you or to carve your name in wood?

Cowboy Cookout Barbecue ⑭
It was here in this massive old barn that everyone from Thunder Mesa and Cottonwood Creek — cowboys, farmers and cattle breeders included — got together for their huge barbecues. It still has the original friendly atmosphere — furnished with unmatched tables and chairs, brought in by everyone and decorated with an assortment of different blankets, barrels and tools.

As soon as the fine weather arrives, the sliding doors are opened up, and savoury smells of the barbecue waft outside the barn.

Take your pick of chicken, pork spareribs and hamburgers at the

counter. Corn, chili con carne and apple pies will be brought to you by men in faded jeans and chequered shirts, and women in long skirts. Two carts re-created from the old West, brimming with garnishes and seasonings, are handily placed in the middle of the room. You may find a table by the fireplace or you might like to sit on the big terrace surrounded by a flower garden.

And then, just to round things off, **The Cowhand Band** has brought along a few instruments. Dressed in Stetsons, chaps, dusters and spurs, they play a medley of old cowboy songs — *Don't Fence Me In*, *Back In the Saddle Again* and many others, plus a wide range of country music. It's just like the good old days...

Frontierland Depot ❾ If you hop on a train at Main Street Station, this will be your first stop. The small station and its water tower are built from timber. There's a stationmaster's office, potbelly stove and a real telegraph; train timetables are posted on the wall on the other side of the track, and next to the freight depot there's an old water tank waiting to fill up the next steam train.

The Cowhand Band playing cowboy songs and country western music.

Chariot Gourmand. The **Railroad Spike Potatoes Cart** was inspired by the old chuck wagons that accompanied the cattle drives.

Some rather unusual kitchen hands will offer you their specialty, baked potatoes — which they take from the oven with a pair of tongs — accompanied by a range of hot sauces and a choice of seasonings.

Judge their dexterity for yourself as they juggle the railroad spikes they use as skewers!

There are all kinds of people in Thunder Mesa, and it certainly has some eccentric folks. You're liable to bump into all sorts of interesting characters...

The **Card Shark** can be recognised by his bowler hat and loud chequered waistcoat. He's an incorrigible card shark and will amaze you with his incredible card tricks.

Gunfighters Stunt Show reminds us that things occasionally heat up in town. The bank has just been robbed, and the sheriff, his deputy at his side, has spotted the bandits. It soon turns into a regular shootout between the lawmen and the outlaws, who don't intend to give up easily. Watch out when you hear the shooting start!

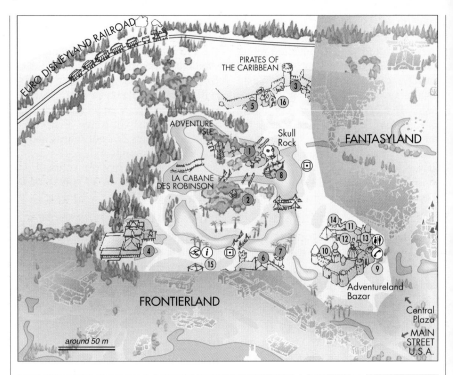

PIRATES OF
THE CARIBBEAN

EURO DISNEYLAND RAILROAD

ADVENTURE
ISLE

Skull
Rock

FANTASYLAND

LA CABANE
DES ROBINSON

Adventureland
Bazar

FRONTIERLAND

Central
Plaza

MAIN
STREET
U.S.A.

around 50 m

ATTRACTIONS

① Adventure Isle
② La Cabane des
   Robinson
③ Pirates of the
   Caribbean

RESTAURANTS

④ Explorers Club
⑤ Blue Lagoon Restaurant
⑥ Aux Épices Enchantées
   Restaurant
⑦ Café de la Brousse
⑧ Captain Hook's Galley

SHOPS

⑨ Adventureland Bazar
⑩ La Girafe Curieuse
⑪ La Reine des Serpents
⑫ Les Trésors de
   Schéhérazade
⑬ L'Échoppe d'Aladin
⑭ Le Chant des Tam-Tams
⑮ Trader Sam's Jungle
   Boutique
⑯ Le Coffre du Capitaine

Adventureland

Adventureland — strange and exotic, a land of fun and excitement. There's the Bazar inspired by the stories of the "Arabian Nights", a mysterious tropical island, La Cabane des Robinson perched high atop a 27-m tree, and the unforgettable spectacle of buccaneers attacking a port, plunging voyagers headlong into the action. But of course that's not all... There are also three very special restaurants, superb shops, carts with sandwiches and snacks, and music at every crossroads. One thing's for sure — Adventureland is the place to take you away from it all!

You'll find lots to do in Adventureland — a whole land to be explored.

The islands are dedicated to adventure... You'll climb a tree, cross suspended bridges, clamber down into caves, find your way out of the maze... and much more!

Adventureland Bazar  You'll enter Adventureland through the large gateway of the Bazar. Strolling through the heart of this ancient marketplace, encircled by thick stone walls crowned with multicoloured onion-shaped domes, you'll be enthralled by the traders' frenzied activity and the skill of the craftsmen working in front of your very eyes. You'll wander down winding alleys, underneath balconies on either side, and past private courtyards with splashing fountains. With each step, you're moving deeper into the exotic world of the Thousand and One Nights. The rows of stalls conjure up the fabulous exploits of Sinbad, unveil Aladdin's secrets, and offer you Ali Baba's treasure.

A genie could appear from any one of

Straight out of the legends of the Thousand and One Nights...

those beautiful lamps; and where and when will you see your first flying carpet? It pays to keep your eyes open!

La Girafe Curieuse - Tout pour le Safari ⑩ The giraffe, who lives in a corner of the Bazar, is often around, and occasionally pops her head over the wall to munch on the leaves of a giant tree, and to watch the adventurers who've come to set out on safari or confront the jungle. Hats, shoes, accessories — you'll find the perfect safari outfit.

La Reine des Serpents - Cadeaux Exotiques ⑪ Papier-mâché boxes, Indian table sets, pottery, ceramics, Egyptian perfume bottles and jewellery boxes... A whole range of exotic goods can be found in the enchanting world of La Reine des Serpents, a fantastic creature with a human face and the body of a snake who just loves to display the splendid colours of her coils.

Follow the dirt track and you'll come across vast quantities of wicker baskets, African pottery and traditional wooden objects.

Café de la Brousse - Rafraîchissements ❼ Here, you're in the very heart of Africa. This little hut facing Adventure Island has a unique blend of colours and aromas. You can relax on the terrace with a freshly-squeezed juice accompanied by chicken wings cooked up African style.

Les Trésors de Schéhérazade - Articles des Mille et Une Nuits ⓬ Near the entrance to the Bazar, there's a shop which brings to mind the adventures of Sinbad. In the middle of it, a majestic wooden camel; from the ceiling, scimitars hang ready to face the foe; walls are decorated with arabesques, and hanging drapes conceal alcoves opening onto the starry night sky. A piece of advice — rummage amid the finery because you'll find the chests overflowing with dresses, belts, leather bags and lots more...

L'Échoppe d'Aladin ⓭ Weaving through the Bazar, you're sure to stop short in front of the river of glittering jewellery cascading down to the floor in one of the shop windows... You're in Aladdin's shop. Choose the trinket that takes your fancy under the watchful gaze of a tiger and three monkeys perched on a flying carpet!

Le Chant des Tam-Tams ⓮ The drums beat out from village to village announcing your arrival.

La Girafe Curieuse.

Aux Épices Enchantées - Restaurant ❻ (hosted by Maggi). This exotic oasis for Adventureland explorers holds a special welcome for you behind its facade and baked mud walls. Inside, the decor depicts many of the world's primitive civilizations. You can sit on the outside terrace or in one of the huge domed dining rooms surrounded by a low spiralling wall.

African, Asian and Indian specialties, including meat and vegetable brochettes cooked on the barbecue, can be chosen at the counter. What a treat!

Trader Sam's Jungle Boutique

⑮ Sam is an explorer who has spent his life bartering in all corners of the globe, and his weird and wonderful collection is right here in this small shack. Everything from a stuffed alligator to an old canoe decorates the pyramid-shaped ceiling covered in plaited palm leaves. Many other of his finds (which he's willing to pass on to you) are on the walls — trinkets, seashells from the Pacific, explorer accessories, and compasses...

Explorers Club

❹ This has been a meeting place for many generations of explorers, a place where they come to tell the stories of their adventures and discoveries. This old colonial-style house hasn't lost an iota of its original charm. The green and white decor sets off some of the world's most beautiful scenery, which has been painted around the walls. In the middle of the dining room, there's a huge tropical tree in which some very realistic animated parrots live.

Maps could speak volumes in the days of pirates.

On the stage to one end of the room, Doctor Livingstone will regale you with tall tales of his hunts and travels. This highly proper representative of the former British Empire also plays the ukulele, and sings wacky tunes from the period.

Whether you choose chicken in coconut, the seafood platter, or spit-roasted lamb... you'll be served by a gaily costumed waiter or waitress! And you can purchase your exotic drinking glass as a souvenir.

Explorers Club also has a veranda overlooking the water. It's a good idea to book your table early on the day of your visit.

Adventure Isle

❶ A thrilling and very mysterious island, Adventure Isle is a little corner of Paradise with enchanting landscapes, lush vegetation, cascading waterfalls and deep creeks. It's here that the Swiss Family Robinson were shipwrecked... And it's also where the pirates of Treasure Island decided to set up camp!

Don't hesitate! Cross over the bridges which link the islands with the mainland. To the north, the scenery recalls the theme of Robert Louis

Stevenson's classic adventure story, *Treasure Island*, adapted for the cinema by Walt Disney in 1950. In this corner of the island, many adventurers have been subjected to the merciless laws of the pirates before reaching the treasure trove... You may meet Long John Silver in person, the buccaneer who swore never to be beaten. To search for where the gold is hidden, you'll cross waterfalls, pass through underground tunnels, and sneak past the bats in Ben Gunn's cave while Skull Rock looms over all. Climb through the mouth and down beneath the eyes, but watch your step!... "Woe betide anyone who dares defy the Skull."

After all this, take a breather at one of the lookout areas to get wonderful views of Adventureland and, at night, the illuminated waterfalls.

Walt Disney made a motion picture of the same name in 1960, and it's this story which is the theme of this attraction.

Looking out over Adventureland, La Cabane des Robinson, on the southern side of Adventure Isle, is perched on a gigantic banyan, a 27-m-high fig tree with exposed roots. Climb among the branches and visit the home of the shipwrecked family.

The cabin is built on four levels and has several rooms which, considering it's an improvised dwelling, are very comfortable.

On the first level, there's a kitchen and dining room; higher up, one room for the children, one for the parents and a sitting room.

Everything is just as they left it. The wheel which brings up the water into all the rooms is still turnin; the organ, the barometre, the lamps and the furniture, all hauled from the wreckage, are still intact.

After you've ventured into the maze of tentacle-like roots which spread down into the earth (**Le Ventre de la Terre**), don't forget to take a look at the wreck itself; it's under the suspended bridge.

La Cabane des Robinson.

● La Cabane des Robinson ❷
Johann Wyss's novel, *Swiss Family Robinson*, published in 1812, was a huge success with children and quickly became a classic.

The pirates' fortress, still standing after numerous attacks.

Captain Hook's Galley ⑧

Everyone in the harbour knows that the galleon anchored off Skull Rock is frequented by the island's starving pirates. So why not follow their example and try a sandwich or a macaroon? You'll eat them by a cannon on the bridge, where fierce-looking buccaneers keep their eyes on the tables, as they prepare Captain Hook's Favourite Punch.

Inside Pirates of the Caribbean.

Pirates of the Caribbean ❸

Pirates of the Caribbean takes you back to the days when privateers roamed the seven seas in search of treasure. After you've crossed a deep lagoon where bullfrogs croak and glow-worms glitter, climb into a boat and the adventure really starts... If the prospect of bloodthirsty boarders worries you, too bad — it's too late to pull out! In the calm of the starry night, a distant voice is heard, "Yo-Ho, Yo-Ho, a pirate's life for me...."
You glide alongside the wreck of a galleon on the shore's edge, and peer through its torn sides. The current is getting stronger and your boat drifts towards an abandoned dock close to the fort. In days gone by, this was where the victuals were hoisted up inside the fortress by windlass. Look out !... The boat has got caught up in the rusty chains and it starts to pitch dangerously to one side. Night is drawing in. The distant sounds of a raging battle echo over the water, and you're irresistibly drawn to the scene of the action. The pirate captain is yelling out orders; there are explosions on all sides, the cannon balls whistling over your head splash down in a column of spray and foam. Further on, the inhabitants of the port are trying to escape from the wild, rum-soaked brigands. As the town burns, the arsenal explodes, and you barely get out alive, with only the memories of this unforgettable spectacle.

Le Coffre du Capitaine ⑯ Here,

you'll still see the marks of the pirates' wild rampages. If you put your ear to the walls of this former inn, now transformed into a shop, you can still hear the pirates squabbling noisily for their share of the booty.

Many items here have come from the debris of shipwrecks. Copper lanterns, model boats, sabres and muskets are displayed on stalls constructed from charred beams and planks faded by the ocean.

Blue Lagoon Restaurant ❺ The Blue Lagoon Restaurant is built in a tropical setting on a slope leading down to a beach of fine sand. On three levels, this bamboo cabin is located on a magnificent site facing the departure point of the Pirates of the Caribbean boats. Fresh seafood is the specialty of the Blue Lagoon, and they also serve spicy dishes that go well with exotic fruit juices and a Jamaican coffee to follow. Don't forget to leave room for dessert — it's hard to resist. The waiters and waitresses, dressed in coloured prints and straw boaters,

A moucharabie in Adventureland Bazar.

give you a warm welcome, and add a special touch of "local colour". Swing to the lulling island rhythms and melodies of the **Blue Lagoon Trio.**

Chariots Gourmands. If you're feeling a bit peckish or dying of thirst, then the food carts throughout Adventureland will soon remedy matters. Specialties will be cooked in front of you. You'll find **Character Sandwiches**, crispy toasted sandwiches shaped into Disney characters, accompanied by a variety of seasonings. You'll also come across the **Stir Fry** which prepares a variety of Chinese-style chicken and vegetarian dishes. Take a pause at the **Smoothie Cart** which has fresh fruit juices and fruit dishes. On the **Barbecue Cart**, there's sizzling barbecue cooked to your liking. Don't miss them!

Musicians and storytellers are everywhere in Adventureland, adding to the exotic atmosphere of this marvellous world.

On Adventure Isle you'll encounter a band of pirates who organize expeditions for buried treasure around the Island.

At the far end of the Bazar, near the Aux Épices Énchantées Restaurant, listen for the sounds of the **Tam-Tams Africains**, a group of tireless percussionists resplendent in their authentic feathered African costumes.

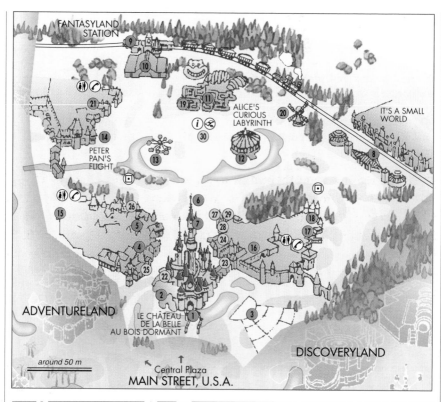

ATTRACTIONS

1. Le Château de la Belle au Bois Dormant
2. La Tanière du Dragon
3. Le Théâtre du Château
4. Blanche-Neige et les Sept Nains
5. Les Voyages de Pinocchio
6. Le Carrousel de Lancelot
7. Excalibur
8. It's a Small World
9. Fantasyland Station
10. Fantasy Festival Stage
11. Alice's Curious Labyrinth
12. Mad Hatter's Tea Cups
13. Dumbo the Flying Elephant
14. Peter Pan's Flight

RESTAURANTS

15. Au Chalet de la Marionnette Restaurant
16. Auberge de Cendrillon
17. Pizzeria Bella Notte
18. Fantasia Gelati
19. March Hare Refreshments
20. The Old Mill
21. Toad Hall Restaurant

SHOPS

22. Merlin l'Enchanteur
23. La Boutique du Château
24. La Confiserie des Trois Fées
25. La Chaumière des Sept Nains
26. La Bottega di Geppetto
27. Le Brave Petit Tailleur
28. Sir Mickey's
29. La Ménagerie du Royaume
30. La Petite Maison des Jouets

Fantasyland

O nce upon a time there was a magical land where every fairy tale ever told came to life... Fantasyland, overlooked by the Château de la Belle au Bois Dormant, is that land, and Alice, Peter Pan, Pinocchio, Snow White and Dumbo the Flying Elephant all live there.

It is a world full of merriment and miracles, where imagination reigns over all.

The drawbridge linking Central Plaza to the castle is your gateway into the heart of Fantasyland. You may also take the Euro Disneyland train and get off at Fantasyland Station.

Le Château de la Belle au Bois Dormant ❶ Charles Perrault's fairy tale, *Sleeping Beauty*, has always set children dreaming, whether they first came across it in a book or through the 1959 Walt Disney motion picture.

Detail of a stained-glass window in the Château de la Belle au Bois Dormant.

The story's imagery-the beautiful princess and the three fairies, the wicked Maleficent and the charming prince, require a fantastic setting. Euro Disneyland Park has created just such a setting with this dream castle. Le Château de la Belle au Bois Dormant is the most recent addition in an illustrious line of Disney castles including the Bavarian-style castle in Disneyland Park (California) and the castle in the Walt Disney World Resort (Florida) inspired by Chenonceaux and Chambord. While continuing in the tradition of its predecessors, Le Château de la Belle au Bois Dormant was particularly influenced in its design by the spiralling, dreamlike architecture of the Mont Saint-Michel and illustrations from *Les très riches heures du duc de Berry*.

Perched atop a green hill with waterfalls cascading down the sides, the castle is surrounded by topiary trees and a moat. The crenellated grey-stone ramparts are topped by pink turrets tiled in blue slate and numerous gilded weather vanes decorated with *fleurs-de-lis*, stars and the Disney "D". The main tower is 45-m high, rising far above the rest of the castle. You may make a wish at **Le Puits Magique**, which is reached by a little wooden bridge.

There is an eye-catching oval window in the wall of the keep above the drawbridge. In the story, the fairies give Sleeping Beauty the gifts of beauty and song at her birth, symbolized by a rose and a pair of doves. Thus in the oval window a beautiful rose turns into a pair of doves before your very eyes. The inside of the castle is simply majestic with richly coloured banners. The hall is more than 11-m high and lit by three large stained-glass windows. Nature seems to have found its way into the building in the form of the enormous stone "trees" supporting the vault of the hall and the gallery above. As you enter the castle, you will hear "wish" songs from Walt Disney motion pictures, such as *Pinocchio* and *Sleeping Beauty*, and your eyes will feast on tapestries, bas-reliefs and sculptures in which the three fairies, Flora, Fauna and Merryweather, are depicted frequently, as well as all the other characters from the story of *Sleeping Beauty*.

A spiral staircase leads up to the gallery, where stained-glass windows, wall hangings and illuminated manuscripts illustrate the story of the princess. There is also a fountain which portrays Sleeping Beauty with Prince Phillip. An open fireplace adds to the enchantment, while the music from Tchaikovsky's *Sleeping Beauty Ballet* floats around you.

La Tanière du Dragon ❷ Deep down in the underground passages, which can be reached by four different paths, you will find a dank torch-lit dungeon. You will also see the sleeping dragon who was picked up by Merlin the Magician while still a hatchling. He lives here, and his task is to guard the dungeon and protect the occupants of the castle. When he wakes up, his mouth spits fire and smoke snorts from his nostrils! So keep your distance…

You can reach his lair by taking the stairs at the back of Merlin l'Enchanteur, by going along the western ramparts, by following the path under the drawbridge, or by crossing a small bridge to the west of the castle entrance.

Merlin l'Enchanteur ㉒ Inside the west wing of the castle, there is a very mysterious shop carved into the rock. It was here that Merlin carried out his strange experiments. His instruments and a whole collection of esoteric objects are exhibited in a hollow in the rock. The stones and crystals collected by Merlin are on offer for your delectation. Figurines made of ceramic, wood, or pewter, depicting knights, magicians and dragons, as well as chess pieces, kaleidoscopes and all manner of decorative items, are displayed in carved wooden furniture.

At the back of the shop, iron gates open onto a staircase which leads down to La Tanière du Dragon.

La Boutique du Château ㉓ On the east side of the castle, the red and green tiling and the spruce trees decorated with garlands and shiny baubles usher you into a shop where the celebrations go on all year round… Christmas, Saint Valentine's Day, and

The castle overlooking the Carrousel de Lancelot.

Mother's and Father's Days. This vaulted Gothic room is decorated with floral motifs and decked out in golds and regal colours which give it a festive air. In the middle of the shop, there is a stone fireplace crowned by a bas-relief of Sleeping Beauty's animal friends. Sculptured wooden chests are bursting with figurines and statuettes of Father Christmas, Saint Nicholas and Santa Claus, as well as little soldiers, dolls, Christmas ornaments with Disney characters and Christmas-tree decorations.

The Queen of Hearts' castle above Alice's Curious Labyrinth.

Le Théâtre du Château ❸

Inspired by the trestle stages erected in the gardens of the French nobility in the 18th century, this garden theatre seats an audience of almost 1,500. Seated in tiers, you can watch either the Disney characters on parade, or relive the wonderful story of *Sleeping Beauty*. On stage, beside a giant fairy-tale book, the multilingual narrator clambers out of a huge inkwell. The book opens, and the pages magically turn by themselves, creating the backdrop against which the characters appear. You will see the cottage in the forest where the princess was raised by the three fairies, the arrival of the charming prince at the castle and the happy ending… It is all truly spectacular and full of surprises. Ask at City Hall in Main Street, U.S.A., and at the information booths for the times of this show, which takes place five times a day.

La Confiserie des Trois Fées ㉔

(hosted by Nestlé). Lost in the depths of the forest, this cottage re-creates the poetry and magic of the fairy tale. Inside, logs support the roof as well as concealing the drawers and cupboards where the three fairies put all their sweets and delicacies. Still more are stored in the baskets and old cupboards. Bent over an ancient stove, Flora, Fauna and Merryweather wave their magic wands and sprinkle magic dust above a bubbling cauldron. But their recipes are a closely guarded secret. Children will love the candy and containers in the shape of Disney characters.

Blanche-Neige et les Sept Nains ❹

In 1937, Walt Disney adapted this Grimm fairy tale for his first full-length motion picture. Since then, it has become a beloved classic and you will rediscover it here in Fantasyland. As you approach, you fear the worst, seeing the dark shingle roof, castellated towers and moss-covered stonework of the queen's keep. Spiderwebs and echoing ghostly voices do nothing to calm your mounting fears. A wagon approaches. Climb aboard, and get ready for an adventure that, of course, ends "happily ever after".

La Chaumière des Sept Nains

25 This shop is divided into two sections by a stream which winds its way across a clearing, with turtles, squirrels and rabbits taking dips along its banks.

On the castle side, in a Gothic stone setting, children will find the prince or princess costume of their dreams. There are jewels and other accessories laid out in open-fronted cupboards.

On the other side of the stream is the Seven Dwarfs' thatched cottage. They haven't yet arrived home from work, but you will find stuffed toys which look very much like them tucked up in their little beds, which are engraved with their names.

Les Voyages de Pinocchio **5**

The adventures of Pinocchio, originally told by the Italian Collodi, were brought to the big screen by Walt Disney in 1940. In Fantasyland, you will share in Pinocchio's adventures and follow the difficult path by which he became a real little boy. You'll visit Pleasure Island, narrowly escape being swallowed by Monstro the Whale, and finally, thanks to Jiminy Cricket, share in the reunion of Pinocchio and Geppetto. And you will be dazzled by the Blue

Pinocchio in the Daytime Parade.

Fairy who, after setting Pinocchio free, disappears in a cloud of sparkling dust.

La Bottega di Geppetto **26**

Why not pay a visit to Geppetto's workshop? This tiny shop is laid out with his bed, chair, workbench, tools and the cuckoo clocks that he makes so painstakingly.

In the window there is a marionette theatre and Cleo, the goldfish, gazes out at visitors. You will find toys, dolls, trains, marionettes, music boxes, puzzles and cuckoo clocks on the shelves of the shop.

Au Chalet de la Marionnette Restaurant ⓯

A brown-tiled roof and geranium-filled window boxes give a Tyrolean feel to this large inn. Inside, a street of balconied houses has been re-created to harbour the restaurant, which is furnished with solid wooden tables and benches, and decorated with beams, wooden light fittings and banners and paintings depicting the characters in Pinocchio's tale. Guests can see the rotisserie where the chickens are roasted to crisp perfection.

The part of the Chalet closest to the border of Adventureland is evocative of a shipwreck, with its curtains made of pieces of sail stitched together, worn-out old planks found on the riverbank and table legs in the shape of sea anchors. You may sit by the fireplace or lunch outside on the terrace.

Le Carrousel de Lancelot ❻

The steeds, ready to set off at a gallop, await contemporary knights and damsels. This is no ordinary merry-go-round. Of its eighty-six horses, sixteen have been specially carved by artisans. All are covered in armour decorated with royal symbols, their manes and tails decorated with gold leaf, and they turn around against a fresco illustrating the adventures of Lancelot. Two magnificent chariots, once part of a turn-of-the-century carrousel, have been restored to their original splendour. The intricately carved organ in the middle is well worth a careful look too.

Excalibur ❼

During a daily ceremony, Merlin the Magician chooses one child out of all those present to go and pull Arthur's magic sword Excalibur out of the stone in which it is trapped. In accordance with a time-honoured ritual, the chosen child, if successful, will be crowned King of Fantasyland. At the coronation he or she will receive the sceptre, symbol of omnipotence, and then, to the salute of the royal trumpets, make an appearance on the balcony of the castle. A document certifying royal status will be granted to the child. The ceremony takes place in the castle courtyard where Merlin may be waiting for you, easily recognizable by his long white beard, his magician's hat and his great blue cape.

Character Shops. Opposite Le Carrousel de Lancelot, there are three interconnected shops hidden behind a row of village houses. Each has its own facade and sign.

Like the first Mickey Mouse motion pictures to appear in Europe, these shops present the Walt Disney characters in a medieval setting.

🎩 Le Brave Petit Tailleur ㉗
The tailor's workshop is littered with scissors, ribbons and reels of thread. Donald Duck, dressed as a medieval tailor, is sitting on a bench amid all the pieces of cloth, making the clothes and hats displayed on the old wooden shelving. Chip an' Dale are giving him a hand while Daisy plays the harp in a corner of the room.

🎩 Sir Mickey's ㉘
In front of this small thatched cottage, like the one in the motion picture *Mickey and the Beanstalk*, there is a vegetable patch at the base of a giant beanstalk. Its stem passes in through the window, climbs up to the ceiling and twists itself around the rafters. Look for the giant's face in the dormer window. Mickey Mouse is fighting the intrusive vegetable, whose enormous pods contain Disney-character toys and games.

🎩 La Ménagerie du Royaume ㉙
This shop brings several well-known characters together in a chivalric atmosphere. Clarabelle, dressed as a princess, is sitting at the window, looking at the passers-by. Minnie Mouse, wearing the costume and bonnet of a maid of honour, is crossing over a drawbridge from a majestic castle. Goofy, in a suit of armour, lance in hand, is sitting proudly astride his horse. Stuffed animals and many other items are displayed on a carrousel.

🏰 Auberge de Cendrillon ⑯
(hosted by Vittel). You've let yourself be carried away by the wonderful world of Charles Perrault, and now you find yourself on the threshold of a romantic country inn. Outside, a small village fountain and Cinderella's wishing well. Inside, wooden beams, tapestried alcoves, terra-cotta floor tiles and pastel-toned flowered carpets set the mood.

Scallops with saffran butter at Auberge de Cendrillon.

There's a large stone fireplace, frescoes illustrating the fairy tale, and the dazzling pumpkin carriage displayed in a glass case. You will be welcomed in the entrance hall by a master of ceremonies wearing a plumed tricorn hat, a long embroidered tunic and a lace ruff, then shown to your table by a host in breeches, silk stockings and Oxford shoes, or a hostess in a pompadour-style dress. The dining rooms, which are furnished in different styles (Louis XIII or Louis XV) and separated by arcades, are an ideal setting for this wonderfully traditional European cuisine: côte de veau, roast suckling pig in cider, rack of lamb... The Auberge de Cendrillon has an outside patio.

Le Troubadour stops by from time to time to play enchanting melodies on the lute while you enjoy your meal.

Pizzeria Bella Notte ❶ (hosted by Buitoni). A mixture of Italian facades, with the Leaning Tower of "Pizza" and a hint of Venice, set in a Tuscan landscape... This is Italy, Hollywood-style, inspired by the famous spaghetti scene in the motion picture, *Lady and the Tramp*.

Bella Notte is a pizzeria with a twist. The brick and stone of the walls, the marble of the tables, the columns and the arches are not quite right: nothing is straight, nor is anything straight-forward. Bacchus reigns over the festive decor of hams, sausages, cloves of garlic, bunches of grapes and casks of wine. The counter stretches out under a trellis hung with old-style lanterns, and the costumed staff bustle around it laden with pizzas, garlic rolls, pasta and lasagne.

The pizzeria can accommodate guests inside or outside on the patio, which is decorated with a mosaic made of fragments of crockery and pottery.

Fantasia Gelati ❽ (hosted by Nestlé Ice Cream). What better setting could there be for selling Italian ice creams than this charming shop? Its walls are painted with scenes from *Fantasia*, and its ceiling is decorated with little clouds in a pastel symphony of soft greens, pinks and sky blues. An array of different flavours and colours of gelati served in cornets or in goblets garnished with fruit is on offer at the counter. You can sample them, when the weather's nice, sitting on the terrace that Fantasia Gelati shares with Pizzeria Bella Notte.

It's a Small World ❽ (presented by France Telecom). This world in miniature has become a classic Disney attraction. It is dedicated to all the children of the world, and it takes them, and grown-ups as well, on a magical cruise across the continents, to the accompaniment of a melody by Richard and Robert Sherman (composers of the music to *Mary Poppins*). This music has been re-orchestrated for Euro Disneyland Park and recorded by the London Philharmonic Orchestra.

The entrance to It's a Small World, a classic Disney attraction.

A stylized facade depicts the most famous monuments in the world, including the Eiffel Tower, the Leaning Tower of Pisa, Taj Mahal and Big Ben. Whenever the giant clock chimes, a procession of little clock soldiers comes out. Be sure not to miss these quarter-hourly appearances.

Time to set sail: your boat glides off between splendid flowerbeds and bushes shaped like animals.

Soon you're surrounded by hundreds of *Audio-Animatronics®* figures representing children from around the world, singing and dancing in their national costumes. You will see Beefeaters keeping watch in front of the Tower of London, Greek or Thai dancers sketching a few steps, children in wooden clogs waving to you, kites flying in the sky above Japan.

After your cruise, you enter a hall housing re-creations of a castle in Spain, a Portuguese tower, a Turkish mosque, the Eiffel Tower and also Big Ben.

This show, *The World Chorus*, presented by France Telecom, is a tribute to the glory of all telecommunications services which bring humans closer together.

In twenty tableaux it shows children from all over the world rehearsing for a concert and using video techniques,

fax machines, and conference calls to work together in the most efficient way. By using these services, it really is a small world after all.

Fantasyland Station ❾ Fantasyland Station is a building in high Victorian style. You may board Euro Disneyland Railroad here (see p. 58).

The C'est Magique revue at Fantasy Festival Stage.

Fantasy Festival Stage ❿ This stage and 500-seat auditorium, incorporated into the Fantasyland train station, hosts regular performances of *C'est Magique*, a Disney-style musical revue.

Singers and dancers join the Disney characters in a musical tour of all the lands of the Magic Kingdom: Mickey Mouse takes us down Main Street, U.S.A., Minnie Mouse plays Diamond Lil from The Lucky Nugget Revue in Frontierland, Goofy goes on safari to Adventureland and the regal couple Mickey Mouse and Minnie Mouse re-enact a scene from *Sleeping Beauty*.

Timetables for the show, which takes place five times daily, are available at

the stage, City Hall in Main Street, U.S.A., and at information booths throughout the Park.

🐭 Alice's Curious Labyrinth ⓫ The

leafy maze in a unique garden filled with strange animals is an

Alice's Curious Labyrinth.

invitation to lose yourself in Alice's wondrous land. When you have passed through the White Rabbit's burrow, you'll find yourself in Tulgey Wood, where the Cheshire Cat, sitting in a tree, will give you all the wrong directions. Some of the openings in the hedges lead to dead ends or up against stone walls; others are so small that only children can get through. You will meet some odd people in this topsy-turvy world, but don't dawdle too much along the way...
The more adventurous among you will set off in search of the Queen of Hearts Castle.

You will be frustrated by dead ends, false trails and worse still when the Queen calls after you, threatening to chop off your head! Quickly, scramble up the stairs to the tower of her twisty, finicky castle. Then go back down the same way, or by the slide. At last, you're safe!

Alice in Wonderland Characters. All the *Alice in Wonderland* characters you meet in the maze (Alice, the White Rabbit, the Mad Hatter, the Queen of Hearts) are more than willing to pose beside you for photos.

🏰 March Hare Refreshments ⓳

You too can celebrate your "un-birthday" at the March Hare's house. This little wooden-shuttered thatched cottage on the way out of Alice's

maze serves fresh fruit punch and un-birthday cakes. You can add sugar decorations and coloured sprinkles to your cakes as you please.

Mad Hatter's Tea Cups ⓬ This large, covered round-about, which will whizz you round in a merry whirl, is based on the scene from the Walt Disney motion picture, *Alice in Wonderland,* in which the Mad Hatter holds a tea party for his un-birthday. Eighteen giant cups and saucers wait quietly while you take your place inside them. Then the platform starts to turn and the waltz begins. A steering wheel allows you to control your speed, if you can! Careful, getting out again may be difficult.

The Old Mill ⓴ (hosted by Chambourcy). With its weather vane and wooden roof boards, its stone facade and its still-turning but dilapidated sails, this old windmill reminds you of the Dutch countryside. Sit out on the terrace and sample its frozen yogurts and delicious marzipan miniatures of characters from It's a Small World.

Toad Hall Restaurant, a typically British atmosphere.

La Petite Maison des Jouets ㉚ (hosted by Mattel). It is easy to pick out this original booth by its pink, purple and blue sloping roof with a weather vane on top. It sells a fine selection of toys and souvenirs. You may also get information and exchange foreign currency there.

Dumbo the Flying Elephant ⓭ This air-borne voyage brings the adventures of the famous baby elephant back to life. All the circus animals used to make fun of Dumbo and his big ears, until the day when, under the encouragement of his friend Timothy the Mouse, he realized that he could fly. Today, this lovable pachyderm sails through the skies of Fantasyland. Climb on his back and fly away under the leadership of Timothy, who is dressed up as master of ceremonies. Waterfalls cascade down from the top of the platform along the spirals which surround this wonderful carrousel. A control lever enables you to adjust your flying height.

Toad Hall Restaurant ㉑ You are invited by the eccentric Mr. Toad to dine at his red-brick Elizabethan manor.

The coat of arms of this noble gentleman hangs above the door; inside, trinkets and paintings bear witness to his passions: cars, aeroplanes, boats... and duels. His megalomania even extends to having himself portrayed in famous paintings, such as the Mona Lisa.

The atmosphere is typically British, with flagstones, polished wood floors, flowered carpets, columns and capitals, leather armchairs and a fine library.

The waiters and waitresses (dressed in green-and-red plaid) are also very "British".

Inside Peter Pan's Flight.

Draw your own conclusions about the specialties: fish and chips wrapped in newspaper, roast beef sandwiches and English cheeses and fruits. You also have the choice of dining on the partially covered terrace.

Peter Pan's Flight ⑭ Have you ever dreamed of never growing up? Of setting off for "the second star on the right and then flying on till morning"? If so, the world of Peter Pan is made for you. Step inside the door of this little house with its wooden, flower-filled balconies. You will find yourself in Sir James Barrie's story, which was made into a film by Walt Disney in 1953 and set generations of children dreaming. Aboard a very special galleon, big enough for six passengers, you will sail through the air with Tinkerbell as if she had touched you with her magic wand.

Fly away over the London rooftops, over Big Ben and the Thames, while little cars drive around in the lighted streets at your feet. Then drop down through the clouds into Never Land, where cruel Captain Hook is waiting for you, and served the Crocodile too, so watch out!

Chariots Gourmands. If you're feeling peckish in Fantasyland, you can always have a snack at the **Pretzel Cart**, where you can buy delicious pretzels, either lightly buttered and salted, served with two types of mustard, or sweet with coloured sugar crystals and served with fruit jelly. Another cart, the **Chocolate & Caramel Fruit Cart**, serves fresh

A lice, Cinderella, Snow White and the Seven Dwarfs, and Pinocchio are all out and about in this magical land, so if you meet them don't forget to say hello. But they are not the only ones, and you may bump into other characters as well...

Fantasyland Fanfares.

Fantasyland Fanfares. The five trumpeters and drummers of the royal brass band wear the colours of Fantasyland well. They announce the arrival of Merlin and other highlights of the day from the top of the castle towers or as they march along in a parade in their blue and gold tunics.

Juggling Jesters. You will be impressed by these jugglers as they send objects flying into the air in the castle courtyard, looking like court jesters in their red, yellow and blue costumes.

fruits coated with made-to-order chocolate. At the entrance to Alice's Curious Labyrinth, you will find a little van called the **Pancake Griddle**, which serves freshly cooked pancakes in the shape of Fantasyland characters, with dried fruit and nuts. **Snow Ball Cart**, located between Dumbo the Flying Elephant and Mad Hatter's Tea Cups, will ply you with crushed ice drinks in cups, with the fruit flavouring of your choice. The **Beverage Cart** offers hot and cold drinks, including espresso coffee, chocolate, mineral water and fruit juices.

FANTASYLAND

STAR TOURS

Central Plaza →

LE VISIONARIUM

MAIN STREET, U.S.A.

CINÉMAGIQUE

AUTOPIA

EURO DISNEYLAND RAILROAD

around 50 m

ATTRACTIONS

1. Le Visionarium
2. Videopolis
3. Orbitron
4. Autopia
5. Star Tours
6. CinéMagique

RESTAURANTS

7. Café des Visionnaires
8. Café Hyperion

SHOPS

9. Constellations
10. Star Traders

Discoveryland

In Discoveryland you'll enter the world of mankind's great discoveries. There you'll see the future through the eyes of history, from man's exploration of space to his investigation of the universe, from the inventions of Renaissance and 19th-century visionaries to his most advanced discoveries.

Discoveryland is full of music, magic and excitement, video images, 3-D cinema, and many outstanding attractions...

"**W**here there's smoke, there's fire...", and you'll see both as soon as you enter Discoveryland. But don't be alarmed, it's only nature's way of letting off a little steam. From Central Plaza you'll see Le Visionarium, a building that seems to be erupting from a rock crater and the surrounding lagoon where smoke, fire, waves and geysers swirl around in a fabulous "spectacle of the elements".

Constellations ❾ Push open the door decorated with the planets, and step into a room where star-studded walls the colour of the night sky reach up to a domed ceiling divided into sections. Each one represents a sign of the zodiac, symbolized by Disney characters like Mickey Mouse, Donald and Pluto. In the centre of the shop, an enormous alchemist's still, made of glass and filled with a bubbling liquid, is surrounded by telescopes and other instruments. Hanging in midair is a bizarre flap-winged *Ornithopter*, a Leonardo da Vinci invention, with Mickey Mouse at the controls. You'll find lots of Disney souvenirs — fluffy animals, games, pens, ties, postcards, key holders, badges, T-shirts, and sweatshirts. There are also tins of sweets in the form of your favourite Disney characters.

Le Visionarium ❶ (presented by Renault). Facing Orbitron is a unique-looking art deco-style building, topped with a dome and five spires shooting out sparks. Timekeeper, the amiable robot in charge of the Visionarium, invites you to live out one of mankind's oldest dreams — a voyage through past and future time. You'll set off on this techno-

logical adventure surrounded by prototypes of a wide variety of vehicles.

An eerie light emanates from the tangle of incandescent tubes and stroboscopes of the fantastic Museum of Invention.

Timekeeper will appear on the bank of video screens on the wall and tell you all about the time machine he has developed. His assistant, 9-Eye, whom he has selected to go on the first time-space voyage, is a little robot with nine lenses as eyes. Using the video screen, she will show you all of the great discoveries which led to the development of the time machine.

Armed with this information, you'll move into a circular room with nine cinema screens in which the *Circle-Vision® 360* process surrounds you with images. Timekeeper gives the signal to begin the voyage, and the charming explorer 9-Eye takes you whirling off through time.

104

Michel Piccoli in the film From Time to Time.

You'll escape from gigantic dinosaurs, arrive slap-bang into the middle of a medieval battle and listen to the young Mozart performing in the presence of the King of France. At the 1900 Universal Exposition in Paris, Jules Verne and 9-Eye have a unique encounter and go on an extraordinary voyage through the 20th century. Their trip takes them on board a TGV and a Formula 1 car, then into the 22nd century, thanks to a futuristic car conceived by Renault.

The cast of this major motion picture, *From Time to Time*, includes *Audio-Animatronics®* figures, hundreds of extras, plus some of Europe's top actors, including Gérard Depardieu, and Michel Piccoli as Jules Verne.

The motion picture, produced on location throughout Europe, uses highly sophisticated systems integrated into the *Circle-Vision® 360* technique to create the computer-generated special effects.

Café des Visionnaires ❼ This restaurant pays homage to the visionary spirit. A highly contemporary decor is created from a blend of bronze, copper, and black and brown granite. In front of a futuristic fresco depicting such works of fiction as *20,000 Leagues Under the Sea*, you can choose from couscous, paella (prepared and served at the counter on cast-iron skillets), or healthy, fresh salads.

You can enjoy your meal either on the terrace or in the glass-roofed dining room. Because of its location at the edge of the Discoveryland lagoon, this café provides a superb view of Fantasyland and the parades.

Videopolis ❷ (presented by Philips). This is Discoveryland's 6,500 m² high-tech entertainment zone.

In the natural lighting from the impressive glass roof, you will enjoy a fabulous show presented on the grand stage supported by high technology video and sound.

In one of the many shows appearing on the Videopolis stage, featuring a cast of thirty dancers, four teenagers embark on a shuttle that will take you on an adventurous journey to the moon, the sun and the depths of the sea. Rock, reggae and rhythm-and-blues music accompany you on your voyage, and laser, fog and special effects create an unearthly atmosphere. The show runs for around 20 minutes and is repeated five times daily.

Between shows, video clips of the latest hits appear on screens. At night, Videopolis is transformed into a huge state-of-the-art discotheque.

Philips also presents two rooms devoted to state-of-the-art technology.

The show times and programmes can be picked up at the stage, City Hall, Main Street Station, or at the information booths throughout the Park.

Café Hyperion ❽ (hosted by Coca-Cola). The largest restaurant in Euro Disneyland Park owes its name to the dirigible floating over the entrance to Videopolis. This 30-m-long airship looks as if it were ready for take-off, with its hanging gondola containing a cage full of homing pigeons, visible through a bevelled glass casing.

Here, as throughout Videopolis, you get the feeling that you're in the departure area for a visionary trip into a future not of this world. Menus in the form of timetables hanging on the walls give details of the different dishes offered (pizzas, spaghetti, sandwiches, hamburgers, sausages and salads).

To make your gastronomic voyage even spicier, you may choose from a number of condiments set out on stacks of luggage. You may dine inside or on the terrace.

The 30-m-long Hyperion *marks the entrance to* Videopolis.

Orbitron - Machines Volantes ③ (presented by BNP). Who hasn't dreamed of piloting a spaceship? A flight in Orbitron is an acceptable substitute. Seated behind the controls of your two-seater craft, you "blast off, climb through the stratosphere and follow your interplanetary route" with bronze, copper, and brass asteroids whirling and spinning about you.

Autopia ④ (presented by Mattel). According to the imagination of only a few decades ago, the great cities of the future were to be interconnected by superhighways along which zoomed ultra-high-speed vehicles.

Autopia transports you into this world. You'll settle into one of 120 "Cars of the Future", '50s-style, equipped with special bumpers, a tail fin, chromed rims and huge exhaust

A voyage in the Star Wars *galaxy with* Star Tours. © *Disney/Lucasfilm Ltd.*

pipes. You (or you and a friend) set out on a future motorway with magnificent landscapes and fantastic future cityscapes on either side, to pass through "Solaria", a city of tomorrow.

Don't forget to respect the road signs and to go easy with the accelerator... or you'll bump the car in front of you! This is one journey that will make your head spin!

Star Tours ⑤ (presented by IBM). "Would all passengers embarking on the flight to planet Endor please proceed to the departure lounge..." This is the kind of announcement you're likely to hear at Star Tours, which organizes intergalactic voyages. From the creative forces of Disney and George Lucas, this attraction offers you an exciting trip into the *Star Wars* Galaxy.

107

The Star Traders radar.

Passing under the impressive X-Wing aircraft, you'll move into the hangar where the friendly droids, R2D2 and C3PO, are working on a damaged spaceship. Video clips presenting voyages organized by Star Tours are displayed on a large screen. The next area the queue passes is the Droidnostic Center, where one chatty droid interrupts his work frequently to talk to the guests. Another droid complains loudly about the "trials" of his job. Then it's on to the boarding concourse and a forty-seat *Starspeeder 3000* for your "flight" to Endor. Fasten your seat belt and hang on tight... because the result of combining flight-simulator technology with film-and-sound effects is thrilling.

The flight gets off to a good start, but it quickly becomes evident that there are problems. Your friendly droid pilot is making his very first flight when an accidental detour requires quick evasive manœuvres. The forty passengers feel all the turbulent action as the cabin moves in sync with the film images and sound. You zigzag between oncoming meteorites and skim past enormous blocks of ice, missing them by a hair's-breadth. And to make matters worse,

you find yourselves in a combat zone! It's the climactic battle from the motion picture *Star Wars*, and your droid wants to join the action. It will be a long time before you forget this sensational voyage!

Star Traders ⑩ The satellite dish on the roof will guide you to this shop. Once inside the glass-and-metal construction, you'll feel like you're about to take off into outer space. You'll find contemporary items here, such as electronic games and toys. Some items are embossed with the Star Tours logo, and others are licensed merchandise inspired by the *Star Wars* motion-picture saga.

CinéMagique ⑥ (presented by Kodak). First you'll have the pleasure of seeing a specially produced multi-image colour slide show entitled *Étienne et la Boîte Magique*. Then you'll proceed into CinéMagique to see an original and spectacular 3-D motion picture from the creative forces of Disney and George Lucas — *Captain EO*, directed by Francis Ford Coppola, and starring music superstar Michael Jackson. The music, an essential element of *Captain EO*, is

Michael Jackson as Captain EO.

Flights of Fantasy. Just about everywhere in Discoveryland, you'll see Mickey Mouse and Minnie Mouse, Donald Duck and Pluto dressed as aviators, behind the controls of flying machines which are meant to take off but never quite seem to make it. These machines are a medley of propellers, belts, propulsion systems, and flapper wings, and look more like flying foxes or insects than airplanes. Occasionally the pilots climb down to let you be photographed with them.

Les Voyageurs. At the Discoveryland entrance, thirteen musicians play "New Age" melodies as well as the theme music from *Star Wars* and other motion pictures. The members of this futuristic group, dressed in copper-coloured costumes, move in synchronized formation creating geometric patterns while they play.

Robomines. A number of almost-human robots inhabit Discoveryland... They are constructed in metal, fastened with bolts, and are fitted with antennae and articulated arms — very hard to miss. You're sure to see them now and again, darting through the crowds on roller skates. Or you might just hear the strange otherworldly sound of their synthetic voices.

delivered via a highly sophisticated audio system, filling the auditorium with thrilling sound. Wearing specially designed 3-D spectacles, you'll follow the adventures of Captain EO and his crew. Their mission: to contact Supreme Leader

At night, Videopolis turns into a giant discotheque.

(Anjelica Huston), ruler of a sad and corrupted planet, and present her with a gift of song. This 16-minute adventure features two songs written especially for the production by Michael Jackson: *We Are Here to Change the World* and *Another Part of Me*.

Chariots Gourmands. Between the Visionarium and Orbitron, the **Sausage Cart** (hosted by Herta) offers delicious grilled sausages served on a rye-bread roll, with sauteed onions and your choice of garnish.
A **Donut Cart**, located at the entrance to Discoveryland, serves sugar-coated mini-donuts on paper printed with a colourful Disney design.

RESTAURANTS	① Annette's Diner	④ Los Angeles Bar & Grill
	② Champions Sports Bar	⑤ Key West Seafood
	③ Carnegie's	⑥ The Steakhouse

| **DISCOTHEQUE AND SHOWS** | ⑦ Hurricanes | ⑨ Buffalo Bill's Wild West Show |
| | ⑧ Billy Bob's Country Western Saloon | |

SHOPS AND SERVICES	⑩	⑯ Surf Shop
	⑪ The Disney Store	⑰ Boat Rental
	⑫ Never Land Club Children's Theater	⑱ Buffalo Trading Company
	⑬ Maison du Tourisme	⑲ Streets of America Shop
	⑭ Team Mickey	⑳ Arcade
	⑮ Hollywood Pictures	

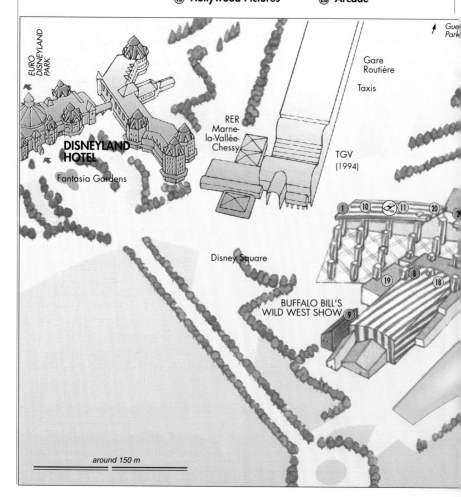

110

FESTIVAL DISNEY

HOTEL NEW YORK

Euro Disney Tram

Lake Buena Vista

Promenade du lac

15
16
4
5

As night falls over the lands that enchanted you throughout the day, a spectacular grid of lights will illuminate yet another world of entertainment. Between the Theme Park and the hotel district of the Euro Disney Resort, bordering Lake Buena Vista, Festival Disney is a sea of lights that beckons and welcomes you to an enchanting place. Theme shops and restaurants will make you feel like you're in California, Florida or Texas. Unless of course you would rather go to Buffalo Bill's Wild West Show for a fabulous dinner show or finish the night at the dazzling Hurricanes discotheque.

Festival Disney, located a stone's throw from the TGV and RER stations, is open seven days a week and is spread over 18,000 m². It contains six shops, five restaurants, a children's play area, a post office, a tourist information bureau, two bars, a discotheque and Buffalo Bill's Wild West Show, which can seat an audience of over a thousand.

One of the delicious desserts at Annette's Diner.

Annette's Diner ❶ "Happy Days" are here again in this 50s-style American diner. Classic automobiles from the period are the inspiration for the decor in the huge dining room. You can select the greatest hits of Elvis, Chuck Berry or Buddy Holly on the miniature jukebox at your table, while munching on a hamburger or brownie served by a waitress sporting a pleated miniskirt. You can also sit at the counter and sip a lemon Coke or a milkshake, or dine out on the terrace. For the kids, there's a special children's menu featuring mini-cheese sandwiches and chips.

The restaurant is open from 8 am to 1 am seven days a week.

Post Office ❿ Although it looks and feels like a typical Disney attraction, this is actually a real post office, and the Euro Disney Resort postman will transfer your postcards to the French postal service to be sent all over the world. Stamp collectors will be thrilled by the stamps they'll find here. A cash distributor that accepts all major credit cards, and a foreign-currency exchange service, are also located in the post office, open from 9 am to midnight, seven days a week.

The Disney Store ⓫ All aboard for the biggest shop in the entertainment centre, specializing in merchandise featuring all the Walt Disney characters. Clothes, books, toys,

The Disney Store: Disney Characters in all shapes and sizes.

stuffed animals, video cassettes, watches, jewellery and souvenirs are displayed amidst various special effects, such as an electric train, rockets, flying saucers and submarines, all tracing the history of transportation.

There are replicas of legendary aircraft, such as the Wright Brothers' *Flyer* or Charles Lindbergh's *Spirit of Saint Louis*. All this is to be found underneath the starry vault reminiscent of the one in Grand Central, New York's largest train station. A word to collectors : limited-series Disney "collectors' items" are on sale at the Disney Store, open from 8 am to midnight.

Arcade ⑳ This game room with a space-age look features an array of video games designed for all different ages. Open from 8 am to midnight, seven days a week.

Never Land Club Children's Theater ⑫ A room for games and make-believe is available for children aged between 3 and 10. Here, they enter an "Imaginary World" through a window to enjoy a few hours of fantasy in the land of Peter Pan filled with toys, games and film. This children's theatre is open from 5 pm to midnight. Your child can spend a minimum of three to a maximum of five hours enjoying this children's playground where refreshments are included in the fee.

Champions Sports Bar ❷ A veritable heaven for sports lovers, this bar is open continually from 11 am to 1 am. You can watch any of a number of exciting sports events on one of fifteen television screens in the glass-roofed terrace. Ballpark hot dogs and

The entrance to the Never Land Club Children's Theater.

roasted peanuts are available to complete the sport-stadium theme. And if all the excitement whets your appetite, you can always order a light meal at the counter, where the names of baseball's most famous teams are engraved. To get you back on your feet, at lunch or dinner time, an energetic waiter will bring you drinks and authentic food such as a chicken sandwich with crisps or a giant hot dog with cheese. Open from 11 am to 1 am.

Carnegie's ❸ This typical New York deli offers Manhattan's best. Try their lox, bagels and cream cheese, hot pastrami sandwiches, corned beef on rye bread, taste the delicious cheese-cake or the superb carrot cake.

The special children's menu includes a chicken sandwich, potato salad and Coke.

113

Carnegie's, which also has an outdoor patio, is open from 8 am to 1 am. A breakfast selection is available from 8 am to 11 am.

Maison du Tourisme (Tourist Bureau) ⓭ Hostesses will tell you everything you want to know about Ile-de-France and the Seine and Marne valleys, and will provide any advice you may need. The tourist bureau also contains a gallery with a storehouse of information about the region's history and culture. There you will discover all the historical treasures as well as the most recent examples of modern architecture in Ile-de-France.

Team Mickey ⓮ Welcome to the stadium! Look at Goofy pole-vaulting over the high bar as Mickey cheers him on. It looks like Mickey's team has walked away with all the prizes. The cups, medals and trophies they've won are on display in the centre of the store. In addition to sportswear, you'll also find clothes in the colours of various American colleges and baseball teams. Footballs and basketballs are laid out in goals and huge hoops, and shoes are displayed on tiered rows of seats. In the dressing rooms, small, medium and large players will get fitted out from head to toe for their next match.

Hollywood Pictures ⓯ Suddenly, as if by magic, you find yourself on the corner of Hollywood and Vine. The set in this superb studio was made for cinema lovers. The folding chair and movie camera are just waiting for the director to start shooting. Books on American films as well as postcards and posters are available in the book section... underneath the spotlights.

Enjoying a boat ride on Lake Buena Vista.

You'll also find sequins, feather boas, glitter and jewels worn by the stars...

Surf Shop ⓰ No one can resist the sunny skies and palm trees in this little California seaside resort from the 60s. Follow the tracks left in the sand by a very unusual character, and give in to the temptation of American beachwear. While Goofy rides a high wave and lifeguard Donald spies on Daisy through his binoculars, you can try on bathing suits, tee-shirts and surfing outfits in the beach-style changing rooms. You're sure to fall for the accessories, sunglasses, sun hats, beach towels, and even the surfboards, while humming a surfing tune under a beach umbrella.

Los Angeles Bar & Grill ❹ This restaurant, located near the shores of Lake Buena Vista, invites you to discover the best of Californian cuisine in a tasteful atmosphere. At cocktail time, or after dinner, piña coladas, margaritas and daiquiris are served with mini-pizza appetizers at the bar. A half-moon terrace offers a superb view of the lake through large bay windows.

After the hostess shows you to your table, you'll be tempted by the varied menu. In addition to the house specialty, wood-fired gourmet pizza prepared before your very eyes, this menu offers dishes such as shrimp, crab and scallops, fresh pasta with smoked salmon and raspberry truffle cake. Wine lovers will choose from among seventy different vintage French and Californian wines to complement their meal. The chef proposes two set menus for banquets and special dinners. Children's menus are also available. The restaurant is open from noon to 3 pm and from 6 pm to midnight. We recommend reserving in advance.

Key West Seafood ❺ The Key West
Seafood restaurant is the spitting image of the wooden shacks and former bootleggers' hideouts that can be found in the Florida keys. Reminiscent of Tennessee Williams' and Ernest Hemingway's old haunts, this seafood restaurant has a spacious dining room and terrace overlooking the lake. In keeping with tradition, the tablecloths are copies of the local newspaper, the *Key West Citizen,* and delicious Garlic Blue Crabs are cracked open with wooden mallets. You can pick your own shellfish by the piece at the oyster bar or order the clam chowder. Don't miss the exotic desserts, such as Coconut Cake and Key Lime Pie, a delicious citrus and meringue treat. As for the younger sailors, a special menu has been cooked up just for them.
The restaurant is open from noon to 3 pm and from 6 pm to midnight.

Hurricanes ❼ Festival Disney's disco
nightclub is just above the Key West Seafood restaurant.
Having climbed the spiral staircase, you'll be swept up into the whirlwind

of nightlife. Hurricanes boasts four different bars, including one in the indoor terrace, plus twenty video screens, cosy corners for talking and a dance floor that's open until 3 am. Don't be surprised if you catch yourself standing there sipping on a Caribbean or Cyclone Special cocktail, dreaming of Key Largo...

The Steakhouse ❻ This roomy red-
brick warehouse, designed to look like a converted Chicago meat-packing facility, houses a first-class steak and grill restaurant.
Subdued lighting, mahogany furniture, a large fireplace and mellow music played by a jazz pianist comprise the charm of this authentic American steakhouse. Having sampled the onion soup or fresh spinach salad for starters, you'll enjoy the roast prime rib of beef or a thick T-bone steak served with clay-baked potatoes.
You can personally choose from the cellar the wine that's best suited to your meal. Try one of the excellent desserts, such as cheesecake, brownies, rice pudding with raisins or chocolate mousse.

Finish your meal with a cup of delicious Flambé Coffee. The children have their own special fare (steak, chips and salad, or roast chicken) as do weight watchers (we recommend the grilled chicken).

The Steakhouse, open from noon to 3 pm and from 6 pm to midnight, boasts a lakeside terrace, opposite the marina.

Boat Rental ⑰ After a meal at the Steakhouse, why not take a ride around Lake Buena Vista on a boat you can pilot yourself? The children will love this unique water cruise.

Buffalo Trading Company ⑱

Aspiring cowboys will find all the trappings of their idols in this shop. Blue jeans, shirts, tee-shirts, belts, boots, hats and turquoise jewellery adorn old wagons in a distinctive Far West setting. While Mickey and Minnie look for gold nuggets in a shop window, Goofy rides a wild bull near the shop's entrance.

Billy Bob's Country Western Saloon

❽ Country-music fans will love this traditional Nashville saloon.

Taken in part from Irish and Scottish songs transformed by farmers and cowboys, country music remains to this day one of the most widespread forms of American folklore. You can listen to it here, while sipping your beer in one of the four bars decorated with hunting trophies, or on the terrace where you can dine on Buffalo chicken wings with blue-cheese dressing and Mexican nachos with cheese sauce and jalapeno peppers served by waiters wearing blue jeans and high Stetson hats.

Singers and dancers appear on stage every night at Billy Bob's between 5 pm and 2 am.

Buffalo Trading Company — with outfits and accoutrements from the Far West.

Streets of America Shop ⑲ "Shop American Style" is this shop's motto. Just a few feet away from New York (where Manhattan skyscrapers, the Brooklyn Bridge and a yellow taxicab house clothes, souvenirs, caps, jewellery and posters) lies New Orleans (where you'll find jazz-related books, postcards, posters, etc.) and San Francisco (where fashionable clothing hangs from the Golden Gate Bridge). You can also buy fine Cajun food, California wines, books, gifts, etc.

Buffalo Bill's Wild West Show ❾

(presented by American Express). This extraordinary show is identical (or nearly so) to the one Buffalo Bill presented in Paris in the 1880s, which delighted thousands of spectators. Horses, buffaloes, cavalcades, stunt riding, excitement and laughter follow one after the other in the ring to create a fabulous dinner show.

The atmosphere of the Wild West hits you the minute you walk into the hall that leads into the big ring, where musicians play traditional bluegrass and hillbilly songs. While you admire the items on display that once belonged to Buffalo Bill, a photographer with an old-fashioned camera will capture the moment for posterity.

First you'll be given a cowboy hat with a coloured ribbon attached to it (showing to which "team", from among the competing ranches, you belong). Then you'll take your seat inside a giant canyon while birds and crickets chirp from dawn to dusk.

Auguste Durand-Ruel, the famous French impresario, will introduce such legendary figures as Buffalo Bill and his Rough Riders from the old West, Annie Oakley, the sharpshooter, and Sitting Bull, the Sioux chief, followed by his warriors on horseback.

Among the various tableaux that bring to life an era which has fascinated each and every one of us are superb parades, sporting pennants and banners, amazing equestrian numbers, sharpshooting and lassoing, Indian songs and dances and an attack on a covered wagon.

Buffalo Bill's showmanship is sure to transform you from spectator into performer, whether you get the chance to enter a shooting match with Annie Oakley, to be a passenger in the covered wagon, or to compete for "your" ranch, along with the other members of the audience, in the hilarious game of trying to get a

Buffalo Bill's Wild West Show: past and present.

"medicine bag" between the tables and into the ring.

This irresistible show lasts for a total of two hours.

You'll dine like a true cowboy at a traditional Western cookout dinner including grilled chicken, sausages and spareribs, corn on the cob, and a delicious apple crumble to top it off. Don't miss this fabulous feast!

Showtimes are 5:30 pm and 8:30 pm. Tickets, including dinner, cost 300 F for adults and 200 F for children from ages 3 to 9. For reservations, see p. 38.

HOTELS

Disneyland Hotel
Hotel New York
Newport Bay Club
Sequoia Lodge
Hotel Cheyenne
Hotel Santa Fe

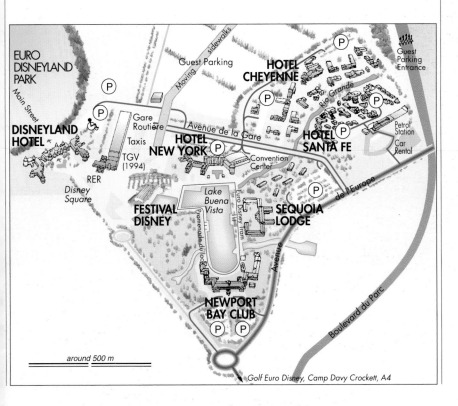

around 500 m

Golf Euro Disney, Camp Davy Crockett, A4

Disneyland Hotel

The Disneyland Hotel is truly a magical place, sumptuously decorated in the tradition of the grand old luxury hotels that graced the seaside resorts of turn-of-the-century America. What's more, its location at the entrance to the Theme Park (a first for any Disney Resort) gives some rooms an unrivalled view of Main Street, U.S.A. and Le Château de la Belle au Bois Dormant.

The hotel's majestic Victorian architecture, with gabled roofs, rotundas and old-rose walls, is one of the first things to impress you when

> A luxury, Victorian hotel reminiscent of the grand resorts that once graced the Florida and California coasts.

you arrive at Euro Disneyland Park. It blends perfectly with Main Street, U.S.A. The central building of the Disneyland Hotel, which has an enormous Mickey Mouse clock on the front, also doubles as the Main Entrance into the Theme Park.

The Lobby. If you are coming by car, follow the Avenue de la Gare which takes you to the front of the hotel. An attendant will park your car when you arrive, while a porter carries your bags up to your room.
The central building of the hotel curves round with wings on either

Disneyland Hotel — spacious, luxurious and comfortable.

In the central building, you will find a breathtaking rotunda. It is an octagonal space, three storeys high, surrounded by galleries and numerous high windows flooding the whole area with light. There is a panoramic view of the Park from a large bay window overlooking Town Square. In the evenings, guests gather round the fireplace in this vast and sumptuously furnished lounge to listen to the pianist.

The Guest Rooms. The hotel rooms and suites, named after Walt Disney characters, are no less magical. They accommodate up to four people in a tasteful decor which subtly alludes to Disney characters in everything from the charming frieze to the furniture itself. The Château de la Belle au Bois Dormant appears on the headboards of the two double beds, and Tinkerbell looks down from the top of the pale-wood wardrobe. A deep-pile flowery carpet and heavy curtains frame the French windows. In the bathroom, a ceramic frieze, featuring the hippopotamus from *Fantasia*, surrounds the bath.

side. The lobby is in the east wing, joined to the central building by a steel-and-glass passageway. It is decorated in the purest Victorian style, with an intricately moulded ceiling and a majestic staircase leading to several mezzanine levels. An imposing fireplace and deep sofas complete the atmosphere.

The swimming pool, the health club and the game room are all located in the west wing.

Rooms are decorated with a combination of elegance and imagination.

121

The 500 rooms including twenty-one suites of the Disneyland Hotel are of the highest luxury standard.

Amenities and services include a personal safe, air conditioning, mini-bar, minitel, colour cable television, telephone, hair dryer, room service, baby-sitting, complete laundry service and valet parking.

The magnificently decorated presidential suite tops the main building. The living room has a large bay window with an outstanding view of the Park. For the prices, see p. 39.

Castle Club. Certain rooms and suites enjoy additional luxuries.

Continental breakfast and refreshments are served throughout the day in a private lounge.

A private reception and information desk, offering an impressive range of personal services, is also available. These rooms command the best views of Euro Disneyland Park, in particular of Main Street and the Château.

California Grill. The setting is casually elegant and the atmosphere convivial in this restaurant dedicated to the delights of Californian cuisine, with a changing seasonal menu.

The tables are elegantly decorated with cream-coloured tablecloths and silver cutlery in a dining room that overlooks the Theme Park. The "open" kitchen, with its large wood-burning oven and mesquite grill,

What could be more fun than having breakfast with Minnie Mouse and Pluto?

allows guests to see the chefs preparing the specialties of the restaurant: maple-glazed roasted salmon, veal chop baked in a black-olive crust with polenta and tomato-basil marmalade, poppy-seed short-cake with mascarpone, and fresh strawberries with rhubarb compote. The wine waiters offer you the best selection of Californian wines. The Wine Cellar is available upon request for private functions of up to twelve people.

Open from noon to 3 pm and from 6 pm to midnight. Reservations are recommended.

One of the hotel's many dormer windows.

Inventions. This restaurant is inspired by the great transport inventions of the century, and is decorated with artifacts of aeroplanes, airships and the earliest motor cars.

You can compose your own menu from four superb buffets, which offer a range of regional American specialties such as New England Clam Chowder, New Orleans Jambalaya, California Cioppino, Florida Key Lime Pie and Boston Cream Pie.

From 7 am to 11 am, you can enjoy a buffet breakfast with some of your favourite Disney characters, lunch or dinner. Open every day from 7 am to 11 pm.

Café Fantasia. Come in and lose yourself in a cartoon universe! Muted lighting and a friendly atmosphere make this little café an absolute gem. The characters from *Fantasia* are featured in the decor: a hippopotamus in dancing shoes strikes a pose on a table top supported by four alligators. Drop in for breakfast, as well as sandwiches, salads and fantasy ice-cream sundaes during the day. Open from 7 am to 11 pm.

Main Street Lounge. Relax in the cosy atmosphere of this piano bar in the rotunda while enjoying the fabulous view of Main Street, U.S.A. Open from 11 am to 11 pm.

Galerie Mickey. This Victorian boutique offers fine apparel for men and women, Disney Character merchandise, sweets, sundries, film and film processing.

Disneyland Pool and Health Club. The west wing houses an indoor heated swimming pool, which opens up to an outdoor sundeck. Why not take advantage of the health club and its amenities too? It offers a training room with state-of-the-art equipment, steam baths, a whirlpool, sauna, massage, a solarium and a health-food snack bar which serves salads and fresh fruit juices.

Mad Hatter Game Room. Young and old alike will find amusement in this game room, located next to the swimming pool.

Hotel New York

Go for the very best in Manhattan. Hotel New York invites you to do just that, re-creating the city's atmosphere in the 30s, with skyscrapers, town houses on Gramercy Park, brownstones on the Upper East Side and celebrated nightclubs. Suites, lounges, restaurants, bars, swimming pools, a sports centre, tennis courts, a skating rink and a convention centre make it an outstanding place where luxury and fun go hand in hand.

> This luxury convention hotel brings the vibrant excitement of Manhattan to Paris.

The City. The central building, Midtown, whose eight storeys make it the highest in the Euro Disney Resort, echoes the harmonious lines of Rockefeller Center. Its monumental entrance porch reminds you of buildings on Wall Street. The lobby, opposite Lake Buena Vista, overlooks the oaks, sequoias, pines and red maples of Central Park and the open-air skating rink on Rockefeller Plaza, which becomes an ornamental pool in the summer.

The four floors of the U-shaped west wing are reminiscent of the neo-classical residences of Gramercy Park, while the east wing, in brownstone, topped by a rotunda, evokes Park or Fifth Avenue.

Behind this building you can make out the domed roof of the New York

Luxury, New York-style, in the rooms.

Coliseum, a major convention centre, in every way equal to its American counterparts. From here, you can easily reach Festival Disney or the Euro Disneyland Park by walking around the lake or by taking the Euro Disney Tram.

If you are coming by car, you will be able to leave it in the care of an attendant before entering the hotel lobby. Two hexagonal lounges, with tiling reproducing the logos of two famous local baseball teams, the New York Mets and the New York Yankees, face each other on either side of the spacious central lobby.

The Guest Rooms. Each of the 539 rooms in the hotel has its number marked on a "Big Apple" on the door. Every room is big enough to accommodate four people and all have a magnificent view over Central Park or the lake.

They are decorated in the elegant style of the 30s: two double beds, a mahogany chest of drawers, big leather armchairs, a lamp in the shape of the Empire State Building on a dressing table with an art-deco mirror, and wall lamps in the form of the Statue of Liberty.

The bathroom includes a wall telephone and hair dryer, and boasts a beige-and-blue frieze around the bath. The atmosphere of New York City is all around you, and all the facilities offered by the hotel are at your disposal (air conditioning, personal safe, minitel, a mini-bar, colour cable television) and the luxury services as well (room service, baby-sitter, dry cleaner's and laundry, hairdressing salon and beauty parlour, valet parking and luggage porters). For prices, see p. 40.

The Suites. Thirty-five magnificent suites are spread over three buildings, thirteen circular-shaped ones in the

Brownstone, fifteen in Midtown, and seven at Gramercy. The two split-level presidential suites are on the eighth floor of Midtown. They are decorated in art-deco style, and consist of a hall, a sitting room with piano and dining area, a master bedroom and a second adjoining bedroom.

Castle Club. The fifth, sixth and seventh floors of Midtown and the fifth floor of the Brownstone offer a series of special amenities. Service is personal and attentive, there is a private check-in and guests can also take advantage of private lounges for breakfast, food and drinks at all hours, an overnight ironing service, shoe-shining, business services and the international press.

Rainbow Lounge. This elegant lounge-bar is designed to provide an attractive setting for an aperitif as a prelude to dinner, or for a last drink, as you sit comfortably and admire the view over Central Park and Lake Buena Vista.

It is open from 5 pm until 2 am.

Rainbow Room. In this luxurious restaurant, you can relive the sparkling and intimate dinner-dances of New York's celebrated nightclubs. The specialties on the menu — Oysters Rockefeller, Foie Gras with Truffles, Veal "Oscar" and for dessert,

Blinis and smoked salmon at the Rainbow Room.

Baked Alaska — are served with the finest selection of wines. After dinner, you can take to the dance floor to the sound of bigband jazz.

The Rainbow Room is open every morning for the traditional Disney Character Breakfast, and from 6 pm to 1 am for dinner and late-night supper.

Parkside Diner. A black-and-white chequered floor, gleaming steel countertop and stools and a piano bar make up the decor of this New York family restaurant. The staff, dressed in red and black, will offer you an excellent range of American diner food: meat loaf and mashed potatoes, thick grilled veal chops, ice-cream milkshakes and an irresistible white-chocolate and banana cream pie... from 7 am to 11 pm continuously.

57th Street Bar. This bar, in the grand lounge in the lobby, offers a splendid view of the lake and is just right for enjoying classic New York cocktails such as a Manhattan or a daiquiri by the fireplace. It is open from 7 am to 10 am for continental breakfast, and until 1 am for cocktails.

Stock Exchange. You can browse in this gift shop for souvenirs straight from the Big Apple: uptown, upscale fashion and accessories for men and women, Disney Character merchandise, sundries, sweets, film and film processing.

Downtown Athletic Club. The swimming pool and the sports club are architecturally magnificent with their large portholes and huge picture windows overlooking Central Park. Within steps of the health-food snack bar, you can dive into one of the two interconnected heated swimming pools, one indoor, one outdoor, play a tennis match on one of the two open-air courts, or venture onto the skating rink (winter only).
At the health club, you can take advantage of body-building equipment, cold pool, steam baths, sunbeds, sauna, a whirlpool and massages. Meanwhile, your children can be amusing themselves at the **Times Square Game Room**, with all the most exciting and advanced video games.

New York Coliseum Convention Center. The New York Coliseum answers all the needs of the business world, both in size (a 70-m-length roof, and a round glass canopy 39 m in diameter) and scope (2,300 m² of convertible space which can be made into twelve independent rooms). This

Relaxing in the whirlpool at the Downtown Athletic Club.

huge complex, fitted with the most sophisticated technical equipment, is just as well suited for a banquet of twenty people as for a conference with 2,000 participants. The wide variety of state-of-the-art equipment is unequalled in Europe. Meetings and seminars may be organized in the great hall (1,600 m²); also available are the multi-function assembly rooms offering various services (meetings via satellite link, security and translation services and office automation). In short, an American-style design for a European business centre.

The New York Coliseum Convention Center — a great place to do business.

127

Newport Bay Club

A refreshing taste of a turn-of-the century New England seaside resort.

L ocated on the south shore of Lake Buena Vista, the Newport Bay Club re-creates the atmosphere of a New England seaside resort at the turn of the century. With its excellent restaurants, health club, swimming pools, croquet lawn, broad porch and inspiring view of the lake, this thematic hotel offers a relaxed change of pace.

The Port. In addition to having an elegant marina, Newport, Rhode Island, has traditionally been the rallying point for skippers and followers of the America's Cup regatta.
It is this atmosphere that you will be recapturing at the Newport Bay Club.

There is an irresistible charm about the large porch, the pale yellow facades, the slate roofs, dormer windows, awnings and pergolas. Imagine the joy of going for a jog around the beautifully manicured lawns or playing croquet with the family. And at nightfall, settled comfortably into a rocking chair, you can relax as you watch the flashing light of a typical New England lighthouse.

The Lobby. A monumental porch held up by imposing columns leads into the lobby.
The hotel reception, information desk, shop and large bar are reached from

A delicious breakfast before a day of outdoor sports.

the lobby, which is decorated in the style of a yachting club, with polished parquet floors, wood panelling and deep-pile rugs.

The Guest Rooms. You will find your room along a corridor lit by oval wall lamps with brass fittings. When you open the door, you will see a luxurious cabin for four.

The headboards of the two double beds are decorated with a ship's tiller, the curtain material is printed with sailing ships, and a sea anchor is printed on the painted wooden cupboard which houses the television. There is a sitting area with white-cane armchairs near the window, and an enormous dressing room connects to the cheerily striped bathroom.

The high-class accommodation offered by the hotel's 1,098 rooms, including fifteen suites, features colour cable television, a mini-bar, a hair dryer, air conditioning, as well as laundry services, dry cleaner's, baby-sitting and room service.

The Suites. The eight honeymoon suites in the tower have octagonal rooms. Those on the eighth floor have magnificent views over the lake and the Festival Disney illuminations. The suite on the ground floor opens onto the terrace. Six other suites include a dining

Sunlight reflecting off the porch columns.

room, salon and living room, and provide sleeping accommodations for up to six guests. For prices, see p. 40.

Dockside & Piers. Large-scale business meetings, cocktails, meals and receptions can be held in four vast convertible rooms, Dockside, Pier 1, Pier 2 and Pier 3. The facility is also equipped with computers, fax machines, portable telephones, multilingual secretarial staff and a personalized welcome for groups.

Cape Cod. Cape Cod, named after the peninsula facing Boston, offers you American cuisine made from farm produce and fresh seafood. A waiter wearing white trousers and a striped sailor's jersey will bring you fresh seaside pasta and grilled shellfish, or a crisp pizza cooked in a wood-burning oven. While you eat, take time to enjoy the lakeside view from your table. In the summer, tables are also set out on the terrace.

This restaurant is open continuously from 7 am to 11 pm.

Yacht Club. Welcome aboard for a gourmet meal in this fabulous restaurant. In the centre of the dining room there is a collection of model sailing ships.

The Newport Bay Club lighthouse.

Sip an aperitif at the seafood bar while you wait to go to your table, and take a look at the shellfish display. You will be able to see the kitchen and the fish tank, and the chefs at work preparing the house specialties such as the "clambake", a traditional New England dish of lobster, mussels, clams, chicken, potatoes, corn on the cob and sausages. The signature dessert is a classic American strawberry shortcake (mounds of fresh strawberries smothered in whipped cream, on a light, fluffy biscuit). At breakfast time, over twelve different types of made-to-order omelettes are available. Open from 7 am to 10 am for breakfast, and from 6 pm to midnight for dinner.

Fisherman's Wharf. It is a delight to have a drink while listening to music in this welcoming lounge, or to take breakfast here, looking out at the boats gliding on the lake.

Bay Boutique. This is your port of call for beautiful nautical gifts and jewellery, Disney Character merchandise, and men's and ladies'

A traditional New England clambake at the Yacht Club.

sportswear. You'll also find all the necessities a seafarer could need like sweets, sundries, film and film processing.

Nantucket Pool and Health Club.
Make time for some fun in the water! The swimming pool and health club are enclosed within a large glasshouse and surrounded by a garden full of tropical plants. In the summer, the French doors open and the pool gives directly on to the garden, the outdoor swimming pool and terraces. Why not try a spot of exercise in the gymnasium, followed by a massage, before relaxing in the whirlpool or the sauna or steam bath?

Sea Horse Club Game Room. Older
children and grown-ups can test their skill on the many video games available here, while the little ones play in the **Children's Playground** outside.

Sequoia Lodge

This hotel evokes images of the famous lodges of American National Parks.

Bordering Lake Buena Vista, nestled between two rivers, Sequoia Lodge is surrounded by magnificent redwoods.

A forest of over 2,000 trees has been planted in this refuge for nature lovers. The hotel is built entirely from wood and stone, in the style of the lodges found in American National Parks.

The Park. Your abiding memories of a stay at Sequoia Lodge will be of forest walks, birdsong or squirrels leaping across the mossy ground. The brown stone and reddish-brown wood of the walls and the grey-green roofs all blend perfectly with their surroundings.

The Lobby. From the lobby, in the main hotel building, you can't miss the garden with its 18-m-tall tree. Depending on the time of year, either take a turn on the terrace which overlooks the lake, or settle into a soft-cushioned cane-and-wooden armchair in front of a roaring fire in the main lounge.

The Guest Rooms. The guest rooms are divided between the central building, facing Lake Buena Vista, and five smaller lodges, built along the river bank and linked by covered passageways. Each lodge is named after an American park: Yellowstone, Yosemite, Monterey, Sierra and Big Sur. If your room is in one of the lodges furthest from the central building, you can hop into a minicar. The rooms, which are comfortably furnished, can accommodate a family of four. Each has two double beds with

Traditional quilts and furniture create a warm atmosphere.

patchwork quilts, checked curtains, and photographs of landscapes, lakes and animals from American nature parks.

Settle comfortably into a rocking chair in front of the window which looks out over the gardens, the river and the lake.

The 1,011 rooms and fourteen suites at Sequoia Lodge offer high quality amenities, including colour cable television, a mini-bar, a hair dryer, air conditioning, a laundry service, baby-sitting and room service. The most elegant suite, located at the corner of the seventh floor of the central building, is very spacious and has a spectacular view. From the balcony, you can see the boats gliding on the lake, the illuminated columns of Festival Disney and, in the distance, Le Château de la Belle au Bois Dormant in Euro Disneyland Park. For prices, see p. 41.

Hunter's Grill. This restaurant is a must for lovers of spit roasts... and for those with a healthy appetite! Walk in and see the kitchen team busy preparing the specialties on offer: leg of lamb with garlic and rosemary, marinated pork spareribs and chicken brochettes. Sit down at one of the large wooden tables, with revolving trays in the middle laden with

Feast on spit-roasted meats carved at the table at Hunter's Grill.

vegetables, salads and fresh warm rolls. Or, if you prefer, you can sit at a handsome wooden table near the garden. Either way, you won't have long to wait. The waiters continuously serve the specialty meats from long skewers and carve your portion right at the table. Be sure to leave some room for an ice-cream sundae, which you can create yourself from the different ingredients provided.

The restaurant is open from 7 am to 10 am for breakfast, and from 6 pm to midnight for dinner.

Beaver Creek Tavern. A forest warden will be waiting to welcome you into this casual family restaurant. You can come here for breakfast, or to taste their American specialties, such as prime rib of beef, grilled meats, grilled hamburgers and main-course salads.

The light-brown stone foundation blends in with the facade made of redwood...

The restaurant is open from 7 am to 10 am for breakfast, and from 11 am to as of 1pm. Opening planned for June 1992.

Redwood Bar and Lounge.
Sip a cocktail, while relaxing in a comfortable leather armchair near the magnificent 15-m-wide fireplace. The polished parquet floor, alabaster wall lamps with brass fittings, and trellised terrace facing the lake all contribute to the bar's warm atmosphere.
Open non-stop from 7 am to 1 am. Continental breakfast is served until 10 am.

Northwest Passage.
A back-to-nature experience awaits you at this beautiful rustic boutique that brings you the best of the national parks of America.
A casually elegant line of ready-to-wear for all the family adds a breath of fresh air to your Disney favourites. You will find everything you need in sundries, sweets and film.

Coyote and Buffalo meeting rooms.
Sequoia Lodge is an ideal setting for meetings and seminars. Two very large rooms, also convertible into a single space, afford a total area of 150 m² for meetings, cocktail parties or business meals. Computers, office equipment and secretarial services are available for you. There is also a personalised reception for groups.

Quarry Pool and Health Club.
The keep-fit centre, located by the riverside, offers superb facilities: a hot-water spring cascading down from a large rock, a broad waterslide into the swimming pool, saunas in little wooden huts alongside the changing rooms and a massage room. You can also treat yourself to a whirlpool, a steam room, a Turkish bath and weight-training equipment. The swimming pool covered by a large wooden roof is floodlit from the lawn at night, and encircled by a spacious beach, with a solarium on the open side. Snacks and refreshments are available.

Kit Carson's Arcade Game Room.
Children can sample the delights of a range of video games, while toddlers romp in the **Children's Playground**.

... while the green roofs add another note of colour.

Hotel Cheyenne

If you are a cowboy at heart, you will be delighted by this unusual hotel, closely modelled on a frontier town with its buildings (bank, sheriff's office, saloon) ranged along the wooden pavements of the main street, Desperado Road. Once you have left your car in one of the two car parks, you can start to explore High Noon Square, where covered wagons encircle the "hanging tree" opposite the jail serving to remind outlaws that frontier justice is swift and final. Piles of harvested wheat, rye and barley are heaped up near the windmill, which is surrounded by herbs and wild flowers.

> Hotel Cheyenne re-creates the excitement of a frontier town in the old Far West.

Cherry trees are planted in the orchard, and two scarecrows are keeping watch over the peas, marrows and lettuces growing in the vegetable patch.

The Guest Rooms. The lobby of the Hotel Cheyenne gives you a warm welcome with its parquet floor, wood panelling, beams and open fire. You'll pass through here on your way to the reception desk, Red Garter Saloon, Chuckwagon Cafe and the General Store.

Your room will be in one of the town's fourteen buildings, maybe above the bank, or over the black-

Western-style decor with lamp, mirror and wallpaper.

smith's workshop. Rooms are comfortable, sleep up to four, with bunk beds for the children and a double bed decorated with a saddle and a revol-

ver. The Western-style (buffalo-hide lampshade, horseshoe on the door, rodeo-motif wallpaper and carpet) does not preclude modern amenities : cable colour television with remote control, mini-bar, direct telephone line and a perfectly appointed bathroom. For prices, see p. 41.

Chuckwagon Cafe. This counter-service restaurant is in a class of its own. You can select exactly the meal you want from one of the nine thematic food stations laid out like the shops along a small village street. Each is dedicated to a different food, featuring the Barbecue Pit and Suzy Wong's Wok, straight from the pioneer days of the West. The trucks from the gold mine, crammed with sticks of dynamite, are in fact drink machines; the covered wagon contains salads; there are soups on offer around the well...

Cowboys at the Hotel Cheyenne waiting for holidaymakers.

The Fort Apache watchtower.

With a map describing the opportunities, you can go round and take your pick before paying at a central wooden counter, just like in an old-fashioned grocery store.

Then you sit down around a barrel-shaped table in the dining room decorated with bales of straw, and treat yourself to a cowboy-size plate of barbecued beef and spareribs. The Chuckwagon Cafe is open from 7 am

to 11 am for breakfast and from 5 pm to 11 pm for dinner, and open for lunch on weekends.

Yellow Rose Dance Hall. A wooden terrace stretches out in front of the restaurant, and in fine weather there will be surprises in store for country-music lovers.

Red Garter Saloon. You can have a drink to the sound of country music in this saloon, just like in the Westerns. The setting takes you right back to the turn of the century, and the waiter in his bowler hat and pink bow tie looks like a real card shark. While you keep one eye on the dancers, you can have a Calamity Jane (alcohol-free cocktail) or a shot of bourbon. The saloon is open from 11 am to 1 am. Lunch is served from 11 am to 3 pm on weekdays.

General Store. As its name suggests, the Hotel Cheyenne shop sells everything, so mosey on in and browse around. Here you'll find Disney Character merchandise, Western wear, sweets and film as well as toy guns and rifles for the little cowpokes.

Fort Apache. A stockade topped by a watchtower provides a chance for the children to play on bouncing animals, a slide, a climbing frame and seesaws, while safely sheltered within its walls.

The Corral. Four authentic buffalo-hide teepees re-create the atmosphere of an Indian village for the children.

Nevada Game Room. The twenty-five video games in this room give the older ones a chance to test their prowess in duels... of the electronic kind!

Hotel rooms are in authentic, Western-style buildings.

Hotel Santa Fe

S et amid an arid landscape
of stones and giant cacti,
Hotel Santa Fe evokes the
Pueblo Indian villages around
Santa Fe, New Mexico. Four
cultures have influence here:
Indian, Spanish, Mexican and
American — the mosaic of the
American Southwest. As in Santa Fe.

> This unique setting captures the historical and contemporary culture of New Mexico and the American Southwest.

Against this backdrop, Hotel Santa Fe
arranges its guest rooms into
"pueblos", small adobe-like buildings,
connected by five different and
distinctly themed trails. These trails
represent the essence and *mythos* of
the Southwestern desert, boldly
weaving an element of allegory

through the grounds of the
hotel. The Trail of Artifacts
is a surrealist landscape
strewn with symbolic icons:
Anasazi ruins from the 13th
century, a cactus in a glass
case, the remains of a 1956
Cadillac half-buried in the sand. The
Trail of Water pays homage to the
element that is so precious in the
desert; it bursts out of a wall in a
torrent, flows like a river into a mist-
covered pond, then enters a reservoir
to disappear at last into irrigation
canals that sustain a crop of maize.
Along the Trail of Monuments, one
finds the extraordinary geological
formations that make up the rocky

New Mexican-style rooms decorated in shades of brown, ochre, and rust.

cathedrals of the American Southwest. The Trail of Legends is dedicated to the rugged individuals who cultivated these lands.

And finally, the Trail of Infinite Space symbolizes the relativity of frontiers, exalting the immensity of space and the infinite nature of the universe.

Reception. South of the Rio Grande, beyond the wheat fields, the desert begins.

Here you'll find the Hotel Santa Fe reception, a large building whose trompe-l'œil ceiling is painted to represent the dramatic New Mexico sky. On the roof outside stands a giant "drive-in movie" screen, an icon symbolizing the cinematic potential of this rugged frontier. When registration has been completed, you can then drive your car to the car park near your "pueblo".

The Guest Rooms. Desert-brown at ground level fading through to sky-blue at their roof terraces, the pueblos contain a total of 1,000 guest rooms, each decorated in the style of ˜anta Fe, New Mexico.

You will find comfortable accommodation for four, with an *en suite*

Authentic cuisine featuring specialties from the American Southwest at La Cantina.

bathroom. There are two double beds with patchwork quilt covers, in shades of brown, ochre and rust, whose warm tones are echoed in the geometric motifs on the mirror and wall frieze. A ceiling fan, colour cable television, and mini-bar are included in the room,

and a Launderette and baby-sitting service are also available. For prices, see p. 42.

La Cantina. In an atmosphere typical of the Santa Fe marketplace, you and your family can discover South-western cooking in this very special self-service restaurant. You can create your own meals as you walk past market facades, choosing from the different specialties on offer at any one of the nine different food areas. José's Salad Truck is chock-full of salads and fresh vegetables. At the Border Stop, you can select your drink (wine, beer or coffee), perhaps stopping off at Miguel's Gas Station to serve yourself with a bowl of soup from the petrol pump. Don't miss the chicken cooked before your eyes at the Rio Grande Grill, and the empanadas and crispy bread at Rosa's Southwestern Bakery. You can treat yourself to a delicious tortilla made on the premises and, for dessert, you can try the traditional Mexican "flans" at Home Sweet Home. Musicians weave in and out among the stone tables on the terrace overlooking the desert. The restaurant is open for breakfast and dinner throughout the week, and also serves lunch on weekends (open from 7 am to 11 pm).

Rio Grande Bar. A carnival mood is awaiting you here around the open fire. You will enjoy the cocktails on offer: José's Pick Up (alcohol-free), Tequila Sunrise, Sombrero, Rosita's Dream and Howling Coyote, or have a margarita or sangria served in a jug. The Rio Grande Bar is open from 11 am to 1 am. Lunch is served from 11 am to 3 pm, weekdays only.

Trading Post. Shop here for newspapers, toiletries and souvenirs of New Mexico. Handicraft items from the American Southwest complement this pueblo setting along with Disney Character merchandise, sweets, sundries, film and film processing.

Totem Circle Playground. Children who make their way here, either via the passageway on the first floor of the central building, or through the village, will be able to live out their wildest Western dreams between the totem pole and ring of Indian tents. They will also be able to explore the ruins of an Anasazi village, an enormous grid pattern formed by the low square houses that former inhabitants of the southwest corner of the United States used long ago.

Pow Wow Game Room. An extensive choice of video games for the entire family is available here.

CAMP DAVY CROCKETT

Set amid 56 hectares of woodland, Camp Davy Crockett is modelled on the encampments of the Wild West pioneers. It offers you a close encounter with nature, in a forested setting reminiscent of trapper and gold-digger country. Not far away, services, shops and leisure attractions are grouped together in a village, built in the style of a Wild West fort. You can rent one of the 414 cabins or pitch your tent or park your caravan on one of the 181 camp sites, less than ten minutes from the Euro Disneyland Park. For your entertainment, choose from bicycle or pony outings, re-laxation at the Blue Springs Pool aquatic park or on the sports fields, feasting at Crockett's Tavern restaurant, barbecues, country music and campfires — all you need to spend a wild holiday in the forest, living like the pioneers once did.

If you are coming by car from the A4 motorway, take the exit marked Provins. At the first roundabout, follow the arrows to the entrance of Camp Davy Crockett. If you are coming by train, a free shuttle service runs between the TGV and RER stations and the campsite.

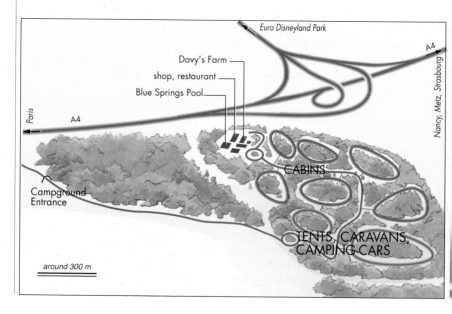

around 300 m

Chip an' Dale are often lured by a tasty lunch.

The reception area is housed in a vast wooden building. Arrivals (from 3 pm) and departures (up until 11 am) are dealt with at drive-through desks. Once you have passed these "outposts", the Wild West pioneer camp is all yours. Or if you prefer, you can register inside the enormous stone and wood-panelled room, warmed by an open fireplace, where an information desk is at your disposal for show times, swimming-pool and shopping hours, reservations and any other information you may need for an enjoyable stay.

The road plunges into the forest, then splits into several loops which lead to the camping sites and cabins, and on as far as the village. To make the most of nature around you, make your way about the site on foot, by bicycle, or in the little electric cars available for hire in the village. Many footpaths, cycle paths and a health circuit for joggers wind their way through the forest. There are also buses offering a free shuttle service inside the campsite and to the Park.

Camping Sites. The first two paths, Wagon Wheel Trail and Cherokee Trail, are set aside for tents, caravans and camper vans. The sites are big

It's never too soon to take up riding.

vision, providing a choice of international viewing, telephone, heating, dishwasher, microwave oven, refrigerator, electric coffee-maker, toaster, and all the necessary household linen. A chambermaid calls daily to take care of the housework. Non-smoking cabins are available. Outside, there is a wooden picnic table and a barbecue, so you can eat lunch or dinner under the trees. A parking space for your vehicle is provided in front of each cabin.

Davy's Farm. On the right as you go into the village, you'll find a little farm. It's a paradise for children, who can feed the hens, goats, cows and piglets before climbing into the saddle for an outing on a pony.

enough to allow you to park a caravan and put up a tent on adjoining sandy ground. Each site has its own water, sewer and electrical (6,000 W) hook-ups, a barbecue and a picnic table. Sanitary installations, changing rooms for babies, a Launderette, telephones, and food and drinks vending machines are housed in large wooden pavilions.

Cabins. Along the other six paths, dwarfed by giant oak trees and lost in greenery, are log-cabin-style trailers, which can accommodate four to six people. Each consists of a living room, a bedroom, a bathroom, a kitchenette, and colour cable tele-

Prices and reservations

• For prices and bookings, see p. 42.

• Rental of a camping site or cabin includes free access to the swimming pool, farm, games area, tennis courts and outdoor shows.

• For the price of electric-car or bicycle hire and pony outings, please ask at the camp information office.

Blue Springs Pool. The camp's indoor swimming pool, Blue Springs Pool, is actually a gigantic aquatic park, covered by an enormous wooden roof.

Everything about it is reminiscent of the Wild West and scenery from movie Westerns: the waterfall gushing down the gold-wash gutters, the whirlpool hidden in a cave, the fountains of water, the slide coming from an abandoned gold mine and the wood bridge linking the small and large pool. In the latter, there are bubble plates and water cannons to add excitement to your swim.

A taste of nature outside the cabin, and of real comfort inside...

The role of sheriff is played by benevolent swimming instructors, who keep an eye out for everyone's safety. And if you feel thirsty, there is a pool bar nearby.

Crockett's Tavern. This restaurant offers American home-style cooking. In the morning you can treat yourself to a real American breakfast with delicious thick buckwheat pancakes or scrambled eggs with sausage, bacon and home fries. For a light lunch, help yourself to the salad bar and a grilled hamburger. In the evening, old-time-favourite roast beef is carved to order.

Alamo Trading Post. Available at this rustic shop built out of logs are Western-style objects and an array of your favourite Disney Character merchandise.

There is also a well-stocked grocery department, and don't forget those "bear" necessities like sweets, sundries, film and film processing. You will be able to shop in a relaxed atmosphere here.

You may also want to linger on the covered terrace for a while, and watch people stroll by from the comfort of a rocking chair. Or perhaps you will feel like paying a visit to the game room.

Sports activities. Why not enjoy a game of tennis, volleyball, basketball, football or "pétanque" (French game of bowls) after a day at the Theme Park?

Indian Meadows Campfire Circle. When the weather is fine, Chip an' Dale will invite you to gather around the campfire at dusk to listen to some country music.

GOLF EURO DISNEY

A superb golf course, complete with waterfalls, boulders, streams and trees, has been created for your outdoor enjoyment. Ronald Fream, known for the championship golf courses he has built throughout the world, designed this outstanding course to resemble a golf course within a garden. Opening in the summer of 1992, the first eighteen holes of the course will be expanded to twenty-seven holes in 1993. Golf Euro Disney is a place to relax and have fun, where unforgettable times are in store for you on the fairway, in the Clubhouse, at the Pro Shop or in the restaurant.

The Course. Located near Camp Davy Crockett and the hotel area, the course is spread out over 90 hectares. Guests will realize as soon as they see the practice putting green, sculpted in the shape of Mickey Mouse's head, that this isn't just any ordinary golf course. Protected from adjacent roads by rows of trees, bushes and grassy berms, players will find themselves inside a beautiful park that includes an attractive residential area.

Golf Euro Disney has been ingeniously designed to satisfy all needs, from top professional players to average golfers. Staggered teeing-off positions have been set up for

Who's the better golfer — Mickey or Goofy? Why not take a chance and have a game?

players of different levels. Paved paths that wind throughout the course were built for the electric golf carts, which are required on the course.

Guests will have ample room to perfect their swing on the forty-position practice and driving range. The large sand bunkers and putting greens will offer them exciting challenges as they progress through diverse landscapes. The course contains seven "par 5" holes in all.

The Clubhouse. The clean, sharp lines of the Clubhouse, bordered by magnolia trees, afford a charming contrast to the surrounding landscape. The vast clubhouse has a domed, opaque white roof in the shape of a giant golf ball. It contains a lobby, Pro Shop, restaurant, conference room, guest lockers and showers, and cart storage.

The Pro Shop. Guests can buy everything they need here, from clubs,

Golf Euro Disney isn't exactly your typical course!

balls, caps, clothing and other accessories to Disney stuffed animals and souvenirs. Golf clubs, carts and shoes are available for rental. The Pro Shop is the place to pay green fees and make tee-time reservations.

The Clubhouse Restaurant. This circular-shaped restaurant offers a breathtaking view of the golf course. Guests will enjoy a lunch of grilled meat, steamed seafood and fresh vegetables, or "tee time" on the patio overlooking the Mickey Mouse head sculpted on the practice putting green. The bar and restaurant are open continuously from 8 am to 11 pm.

Operating hours and fees

Golf Euro Disney is open from 8 am, seven days a week, 365 days a year.

Green fees, including golf cart, are approximately 550 F per round on weekends and 385 F during the week. Group rates, as well as packages (Golf + Lunch/Golf + Dinner), are available. Golf clubs can be rented for 100 F per round.

Less-expensive "twilight" green fees are also offered. Inquire at the Pro Shop.

RESTAURANT INDEX

Restaurants classified by type of cuisine

Restaurants classified by number of castles

INDEX

Printed and Bound in France
by Partenaires S.A.

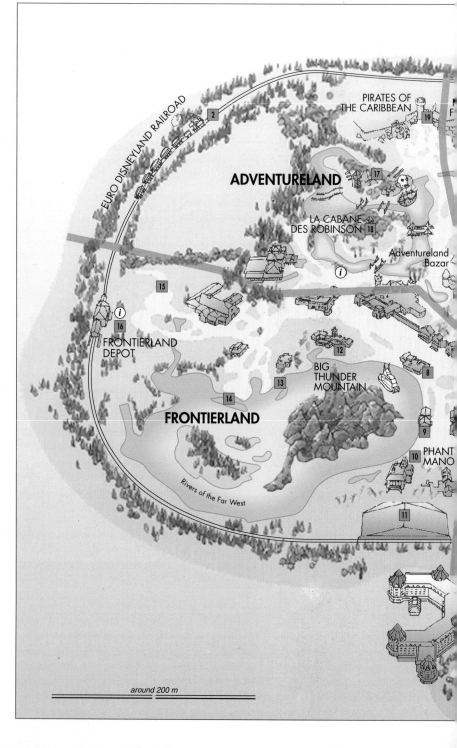

PIRATES OF
THE CARIBBEAN

19

F

ADVENTURELAND

17

LA CABANE
DES ROBINSON   18

Adventureland
Bazar

EURO DISNEYLAND RAILROAD

2

i

15

16

i

FRONTIERLAND
DEPOT

12

13

BIG
THUNDER
MOUNTAIN

8

14

FRONTIERLAND

9

10

PHANT
MANO

Rivers of the Far West

11

around 200 m